KT-171-466

The author wishes to thank the following
for their advice and help:

Dr Mark Hassall of the Institute
of Archaeology

Dr Demetrios Michaelides of the
British School of Archaeology at Rome

Mr John Lowe who supplied many photographs
and translations of Italian articles

First published 1979
Macdonald Educational Ltd
Holywell House
Worship Street
London EC2A 2EN

ISBN 0 356 06303 8

© Peter Connolly, 1979

Made and printed by
Morrison and Gibb Limited
Edinburgh, Scotland

POMPEII

Written and illustrated by
Peter Connolly

Macdonald Educational

Introduction

In the first century AD the whole of western Europe, the Near East and North Africa was ruled by Rome. Italy had become rich. The bay of Naples was a prosperous centre of trade with a score of small towns stretched along its shores. Many wealthy Romans had built villas overlooking the sea. Hundreds of these covered the lower slopes of Vesuvius, the cone-shaped mountain that dominated the bay. At the north-western tip of the bay was the great naval base of Misenum.

The morning of 24 August AD 79 was just another summer's day. In the town of Pompeii tradesmen removed the shutters from their shops and hung up their merchandise. The morning passed without event. Lunch was being prepared in the laundry of Stephanus. A group of gladiators met in a bar. They put down the equipment they had been carrying and sipped their hot wine. Modestus, the baker, stoked his oven and carefully placed the dough alongside the flames.

Suddenly the air was split by a resounding crash, and the ground shook. People rushed into the streets. Most of them could not see what had happened. Then fragments of charred stone started to fall out of the clear blue sky. Those out in the open would have seen the great column of smoke rising from Mount Vesuvius. Pieces of pumice began to rattle down the roofs and into the streets. The sky became overcast and darkness descended. Within hours Pompeii and a number of other towns were buried under several metres of pumice and ashes. Most of the population fled when the eruption started. About two thousand stayed in Pompeii and were entombed there. Countless thousands of others died in the countryside. This was the greatest natural disaster in European history.

The first part of this book describes briefly the destruction and excavation of Pompeii. It goes on to look at the town and its history. The main part of the book examines one small area of Pompeii and reconstructs its houses and shops, relating them to the people who lived there. It also takes a look at the places of relaxation and entertainment — the baths, the theatres and the amphitheatre.

Contents

The disaster

24 August AD 79: afternoon

Gaius Plinius Secundus (Pliny the Elder) was admiral of the Roman fleet at Misenum. His nephew, Pliny the Younger, who was about seventeen years old, was staying with him.

It was early afternoon when the admiral's wife drew his attention to a large cloud hanging over the eastern side of the bay. Years later the younger Pliny related the succeeding events in his famous letters to the historian Tacitus. He compared the large cloud to an umbrella pine which rose to a great height on a sort of trunk and then split off into branches. The admiral, who had written a large work on natural history, could hardly contain his curiosity. He called for a boat and prepared to sail across the bay for a closer look. As he was leaving he received a message from the wife of a friend who lived at the foot of Vesuvius. She begged him to come to her rescue as all routes of escape by land were cut off. The admiral immediately ordered out the fleet and set off across the bay.

The fleet headed directly for Vesuvius. As they approached ashes began to float down. Soon bits of pumice and blackened stones were landing on the deck. It was impossible to reach the shore as it was blocked by debris. By this time Pompeii was already buried. Pliny's sailors begged him to turn back but instead he turned south to Stabiae.

24 August AD 79: evening

At Stabiae they managed to get ashore. Here Pliny was met by another friend, Pomponianus, who had also been unable to escape by land. The sea was now too rough for them to recross the bay. Night was falling so they decided to wait until morning. The admiral bathed and dined. After reassuring his friends he went to bed. The rest of them sat up. During the night, the hail of pumice and ashes continued and began to pile up in the courtyard outside Pliny's bedroom. Shortly before dawn his friends roused him for fear that he might be trapped in his room.

25 August AD 79: dawn

Although morning had arrived it was still pitch black. The admiral and his companions went down to the shore with torches and lamps. They tied cushions over their heads as a protection against the hail of pumice, for, although the pumice was light and porous, it could hurt.

The sea was still too rough to launch the galleys. The old admiral was suffering greatly from the poisonous fumes. They laid a sheet out on the ground for him to rest. Repeatedly he asked for water. When finally they helped him to his feet he collapsed and died.

Daylight did not return for two days. Only then was it possible to see the full extent of the disaster.

Pompeii, which was right in the middle of the volcanic fallout, was buried under 3-5 metres of ash and pumice. The illustration shows the effect of the first few minutes of the hail of pumice.

Vesuvius

A Pompeian painting believed to show Vesuvius found in the House of the Centenary.

The return of daylight

The return of daylight revealed the extent of the disaster. The great cone of Vesuvius was now a ragged stump. Almost the whole of the southern end of the bay had been buried. Along the southern and western slopes of Vesuvius, where so many great villas had stood, was a grey wilderness. Several towns had disappeared including Herculaneum, Pompeii, Stabiae, Oplontis and Taurania. Where Pompeii had once stood only the tops of the buildings still standing rose above the ashes.

The earthquake

To those who lived around the bay Vesuvius was just a large hill. Even Strabo the geographer, who recognized its true nature and described its burnt crater, did not realize that it was still active. In the eighth century BC the volcano had been very active, but it had lain dormant for eight hundred years. A thick layer of lava had hardened to form a plug in the crater. By the first century AD pressure had grown within the cone as the volcano tried to find a new outlet. On 5 February AD 62 southern Italy was shaken by violent earthquakes as the gases tried to force their way out.

Vesuvius seen from the hills above Stabiae. Pompeii lies in front of the mountain and Herculaneum to the left.

The eruption

Seventeen years later the pressure had again built up. For four days there had been earth tremors. Streams around Vesuvius had dried up. On the morning of 24 August AD 79 the pressure of the gases finally blew out the plug. Millions of tonnes of lava, pumice and ashes were rocketed into the sky. This formed the great cloud that Pliny described. The cloud drifted southwards straight across to Pompeii where the fallout was worst. By the time that Pliny reached Stabiae Pompeii had been buried for several hours. It is estimated that about two thousand people died within the town. There must have been many more thousands of bodies scattered across the countryside.

Pompeii was buried under three to five metres of pumice and ashes. Herculaneum, which was outside the fallout area, suffered an even worse fate. During the eruption torrential rain and condensing steam from the volcano combined with the ashes on the mountainside. This flowed down the mountain and buried Herculaneum under thirteen metres of boiling mud.

After the eruption

The whole centre of Vesuvius was blown out by the eruption. Afterwards the sides fell in to form a vast crater more than eleven kilometres in circumference. Since AD 79 a new cone has formed on the south side. The north-east wall of the old crater still exists under the name Monte Somma.

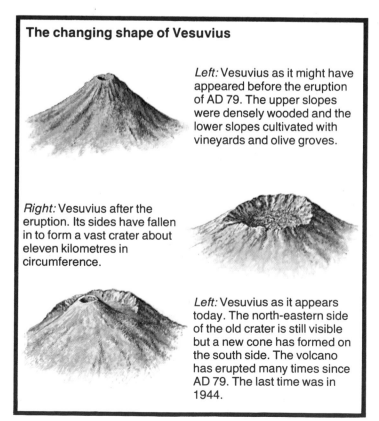

The changing shape of Vesuvius

Left: Vesuvius as it might have appeared before the eruption of AD 79. The upper slopes were densely wooded and the lower slopes cultivated with vineyards and olive groves.

Right: Vesuvius after the eruption. Its sides have fallen in to form a vast crater about eleven kilometres in circumference.

Left: Vesuvius as it appears today. The north-eastern side of the old crater is still visible but a new cone has formed on the south side. The volcano has erupted many times since AD 79. The last time was in 1944.

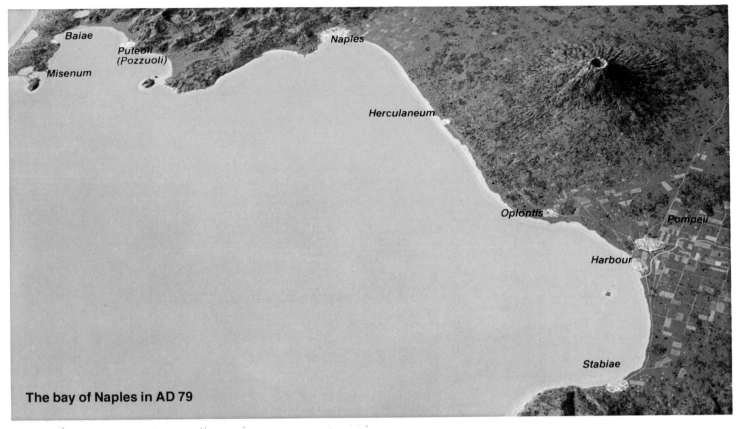

Baiae
Puteoli
(Pozzuoli)
Misenum
Naples
Herculaneum
Oplontis
Pompeii
Harbour
Stabiae

The bay of Naples in AD 79

Herculaneum
Pompeii
Stabiae

Vesuvius seen from the west showing the Pompeian plain and the hills behind Stabiae. The reconstruction shows the great cloud described by Pliny which drifted southwards burying the Pompeian plain. The summit of Vesuvius is about ten kilometres from Pompeii and seven from Herculaneum.

4m
Top soil
Lapilli
Ash
Lapilli
Ash
3
Sandy ash with carbonized wood
Lapilli
2
Hardened volcanic sand
Greenish grey pumice
Heavier grey pumice
1
Light white pumice
Lava pebbles
0

Left: A section of the volcanic fallout that covered Pompeii. The section was taken at the large *Palaestra* next to the amphitheatre. Here the covering was three and a half metres deep.

Right: Map of the Bay of Naples showing the fallout area. The dark grey shows the densest area of fallout (more than two metres) the mid-grey, one to two metres, and the lightest grey, half to one metre.

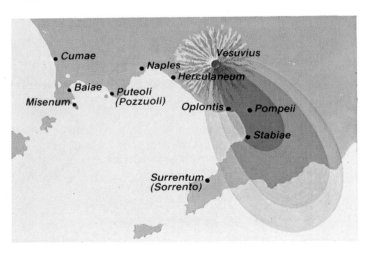

Cumae
Naples
Vesuvius
Herculaneum
Baiae
Puteoli
(Pozzuoli)
Misenum
Oplontis
Pompeii
Stabiae
Surrentum
(Sorrento)

Discovery and excavation

The legend of the lost city

As time passed Pompeii was forgotten. In the fifth century Rome fell and Italy collapsed into barbarism and ignorance. But for more than a thousand years the legend of a lost city lived on.

In 1594 Count Muzzio Tuttavilla decided to build an aqueduct to carry water from the river Sarno to his villa at Torre Annunziata at the foot of Vesuvius. As the workmen were digging along the southern slopes of the volcano they uncovered ruined buildings. They even turned up an inscription on which was written *decurio Pompeis*. This inscription, which referred to a town councillor (*decurion*) at Pompeii, was believed to come from a villa belonging to Pompey the Great. The matter was soon forgotten. A century later a well was being dug when once again inscriptions were brought to the surface, including one that referred to Pompeii. Again nothing was done.

Herculaneum and Pompeii are found

In spite of these two discoveries Pompeii was not the first of the buried towns to be excavated. In 1710, thirteen kilometres further up the coast at Resina, a peasant was digging another well in which he discovered large slabs of marble. A local nobleman seeing the marbles realized at once what they were and bought the land. Herculaneum, one of the buried towns had been discovered. A great treasure hunt began.

For nearly forty years Herculaneum was robbed. Its treasures went to adorn noble houses. When this excavation proved difficult people remembered the other finds. On 23 March 1748 digging began at Pompeii.

For more than a hundred years the excavations proceded in a haphazard way. They depended entirely on the whims of the kings of Naples who changed regularly as Austria, Spain and France vied for power in Italy.

Fiorelli takes over the excavations

In 1860 Garibaldi united Italy and the struggle for power in Naples ended. Guiseppe Fiorelli was appointed Professor of Archaeology at Naples and took over control of the excavations. It was to this man more than any other that the scientific excavation of Pompeii was due.

Fiorelli cleared away the mounds of earth that littered the site. These mounds had been moved backwards and forwards as the excavators wanted to dig new areas. He cleared the streets so that one could see a plan of the town. He divided the site up into numbered regions. Then, using the street plan, he numbered each area that was surrounded by streets calling these *insulae* (islands). These are equivalent to the blocks in a modern town. Each doorway was also numbered so that every house and shop could be identified. For example, the house of Lucius Ceius Secundus is in region I, *insula* 6, doorway number 15.

Fiorelli's excavation journals

Now for the first time detailed accounts of the excavations were kept. These listed the site where an object was found, its position within the site and its depth in the ground. It also stated any conclusions that might be drawn from this. Fiorelli insisted that wherever possible things should be left in position within the houses. Prior to this all valuables had been removed to form great collections; paintings had been prised off walls and mosaics ripped from floors. It is a great tragedy that today so many of the priceless treasures of Pompeii are stolen by unscrupulous collectors. Some tourists even break off pieces from objects as souvenirs.

Perhaps Fiorelli is best remembered for his plaster casts of the dead. Many skeletons were found at Pompeii. The fascinating thing was not so much the skeleton as the imprint of the body which was shown in the ashes. When people who were caught by the eruption died, the ashes and pumice settled around their bodies. Then the rain came which washed more ash down to fill in the cracks between the pumice stones. This then hardened to seal in the bodies. In time the flesh and clothing decayed and disappeared leaving only the bones, but every detail of the body was imprinted in the ashes. Fiorelli invented a method of casting copies of the bodies by pumping a type of plaster into the cavity left by the body. This process has since been used to cast doors, shutters and even tree roots.

The process was used to fill a cavity discovered during the excavation of the house of Vesonius Primus. When the plaster cast was taken out it was found to be a dog complete with collar (see right). It had been tethered by a chain in the *atrium* of the house. As the ashes had come in through the opening in the roof they gradually began to fill the room. The poor creature had climbed up higher and higher until his chain was stretched taut. Then, still struggling to get free, he had been buried alive.

The later excavations

Since Fiorelli's time the technique of excavation has continued to improve. The buildings of Pompeii were generally crushed by the weight of the pumice and ashes. The tops of those buildings which remained standing and protruded above the ashes were robbed for building materials by later generations. One seldom finds a building higher than about four metres. Many buildings have now been restored with reconstructed roofs, so today one can enter a building and get an idea of what it must have been like.

Above: The excavations at the rear of the house of Marcus Lucretius region 1, *insula* 6, no. 2. The garden is being excavated. Several bodies were found here (see p.48).

Below: Fiorelli's process. When a body is discovered plaster is pumped into the cavity so that the original shape of the victim can be cast.

Right: The cast of Primus' dog which died in agony, its head pulled down by the chain with which it was tethered.

Below: The plaster cast of the body shown above. Notice the clear impression of his sandals.

Left: A copy of folding doors made by Fiorelli's process. These are from the Villa of the Mysteries. Window shutters and door posts have been cast by this method during the recent excavation of the Villa of Poppaea at Torre Annunziata.

Overleaf: An aerial view of the excavations at Pompeii. The picture is taken from the south. Centre left is the forum and bottom right the two theatres.

13

Aerial view of the excavations

The town and its history

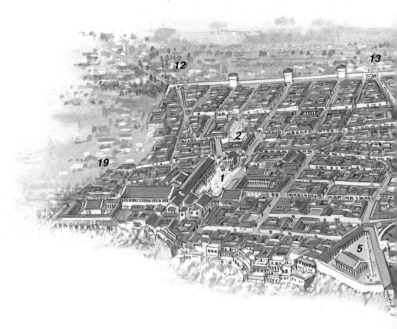

The position and layout of Pompeii

About four-fifths of Pompeii have now been uncovered. This is enough to give us an idea of what the town looked like (see reconstruction on right). On the left (west) side is the forum with the temples and municipal buildings grouped around it. In the foreground is the large theatre and on the right the amphitheatre. The rest is occupied mainly by houses. Outside the gates are cemeteries.

The town was built on a prehistoric lava flow which ends in a steep cliff. This gives the south-west side of the town excellent defences. The town was about 500 metres from the sea. The eruption of 79 filled up the bay and Pompeii is now about two kilometres inland. It had a circuit wall of about three kilometres, pierced by eight gates. Towers were built at the weakest points on the north and east. After the establishment of the 'Roman peace', the walls were demolished at the south-west corner and terraced houses with a fine sea view were built into the cliff face. On the coast was the port of Pompeii. Although some buildings have been found the site of the port has not been definitely identified.

The oldest building in Pompeii is sixth century BC. At this time the town probably consisted only of the small area in the south-west corner bounded by the main forum (*1*) and the triangular forum (*5*). From here the town gradually spread out towards the north and east (see p.74).

The history of the town

Pompeii had a varied history, controlled successively by Greeks, Etruscans, Samnites and finally Romans. The Romans captured it during the second Samnite war at the end of the fourth century BC. In accordance with normal Roman practice Pompeii was allowed to govern itself but owed allegiance to Rome.

Two hundred years later the Italians revolted against Rome. Pompeii, Stabiae and Herculaneum joined the revolt. The Roman general Sulla recaptured the three towns. Stabiae was destroyed and Pompeii was turned into a Roman colony. Many of the inhabitants were turned out to make room for the new settlers.

Most of Pompeii's remains date from the period which followed the establishment of the colony (80 BC). The old and the new inhabitants of Pompeii gradually mixed and the town once again became a single unit with a large degree of self-government. The vigour with which the elections of local magistrates were pursued is evident from the large number of election posters painted on the walls of houses.

In the first century BC the bay became a popular resort for wealthy Romans. Many great villas (country houses) were built along the slopes of Vesuvius. The Roman orator Cicero had a villa at Pompeii.

Below: A tower west of the Vesuvius Gate. These towers were three storeys high. The town defences consisted of two walls about six metres apart. The space between them was filled with rubble and earth. In most places the walls are made of large blocks of stone.

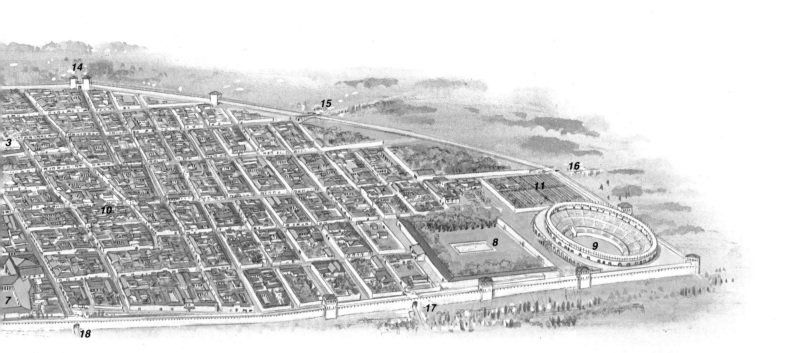

Above: A reconstructed aerial view of Pompeii from the south.
1 The forum
2 The forum baths
3 The central baths
4 The Stabian baths
5 The triangular forum
6 The large theatre
7 The gladiators' barracks
8 The Great Palaestra
9 The amphitheatre
10 Region I, insula 6
11 Vineyard
12 The Herculaneum Gate
13 The Vesuvius Gate
14 The Capuan Gate
15 The Nolan Gate
16 The Sarno Gate
17 The Nucerian Gate
18 The Stabian Gate
19 The Marine Gate

Left: The Marine Gate from the outside. The passage to the left is for pedestrians. The other is for animals and light vehicles. The incline here is too steep for heavy vehicles.

Below left: Houses built over the walls on the west side of the town.
Below: Tombs along the road outside the Herculaneum Gate.

The forum

The political and commercial centre.
This picture shows the remains of the forum seen from the south-west corner. This was the political, commercial and religious centre of the town. The main temples, the government buildings, the law courts and the business exchanges were grouped around it. At the bottom left is the entrance to the basilica which was a sort of law court-cum-stock exchange. The line of columns across the picture is the remains of the two-storey colonnade which once ran along three sides of the forum. Merchants set up their stalls beneath this colonnade.

In the centre of the left-hand page is the base of the temple of Jupiter and to the right of it is the market. The government buildings were at the south end of the forum. Vesuvius can be seen in the background. When the eruption came most of these buildings were still lying in ruins after the earthquake of AD 62.

The streets and water supply

The streets and sidewalks
The streets of Pompeii vary greatly in width. Most are very narrow, from 2.4 to 4.5 metres wide, while the widest is just over seven metres. These streets were paved with large polygonal blocks of Vesuvian lava. On either side of most streets there was a raised sidewalk, usually about one-third of a metre high but sometimes much more. Large blocks of lava were used for kerb-stones. The space between the kerb-stones and the buildings was filled with a mixture of rubble and mortar. The pavement was surfaced with a mixture of brick chips and mortar. Occasionally a decorative design was set into the surface. Brick chips and mortar were also commonly used for floors.

Dirty streets
The road was usually raised in the centre so that water would run into the gutters. Similarly the sidewalk usually sloped down towards the road. Pompeii had no proper sewage system and much of the waste must have been thrown into the gutter. Large stepping stones were set into the roads at intervals so that people could cross without getting dirty. These stepping stones were placed so that carts could pass over them with their wheels in the gaps on either side. The axle width of these vehicles (1.4 metres) can easily be seen by the deep ruts in the roads. These are especially deep between the stepping stones where the wheels have mounted the stepping stone and then slipped down into the rut. Ancient vehicles were drawn by pairs of animals side by side. This meant that the animals also passed through the gaps between the stones.

Water supply
Originally Pompeii's water supply had come from the river Sarno and from wells. Later an aqueduct had been constructed to bring water from the hills. This served all the local towns. Inside the town the water was carried through lead pipes which ran beneath the side-walks. It was taken to the wealthier houses, to the baths and to the public fountains which can be found throughout the town. These public fountains were where the poor could draw water.

Next to the fountain there is often a water column. These are square columns which once had a lead tank on top. Unfortunately the top is always missing. On either side of the column is an inset for the lead pipes. Pompeii is built on a slope and one must assume that the height of these towers was the same as the reservoir that supplied them so that the tanks could be kept full but not overflow. Just inside the Vesuvius Gate is a small brick building, where water from the aqueduct was channelled three ways. The building was damaged in the earthquake of AD 62 and was not in use at the time of the eruption.

Above: A drain in the via dell' Abbondanza. Pompeii had no proper sewers. Such drains are exceptional.

Below: A water column with a fountain beyond it. It is in the via Stabiana to the east side of region VI, *insula* 14. This was one of the columns supplied by the water-distribution building at the Vesuvius Gate.

Left: Lead water pipes clearly visible where the surface of the sidewalk has worn away. A junction pipe can be seen entering a house.

Above: The via della Fortuna at its junction with the via Stabiana. This picture shows clearly the stepping stones and the deep ruts caused by the cart wheels.

Below left: A public fountain in the via dell'Abbondanza opposite region I, insula 6.

Below: The water-distribution building at the Vesuvius Gate. Here the water from the aqueduct was divided into three channels.

People and accommodation

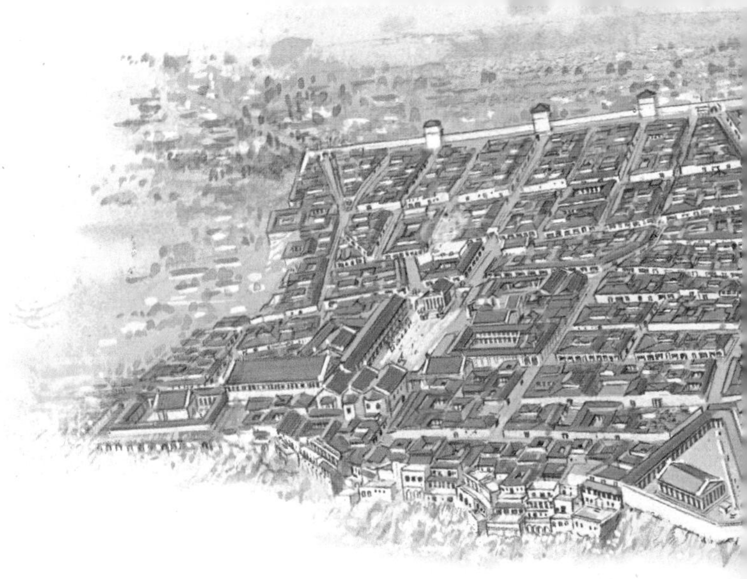

Above: A reconstruction painting of Pompeii.

Citizens and slaves

Pompeii probably had a population of eight to ten thousand. This was about 60 per cent free and 40 per cent slave. Free men and women generally considered it below their dignity to do manual work. In the home all cooking and housework would be done by slaves. The life of a slave could be terrible — for example working in the mines or fighting in the amphitheatre — but the lot of the domestic slave was often tolerable.

Domestic slaves came mainly from the east. They were often well educated — sometimes better than their masters. A small household usually had two or three slaves. A large household had many more, including specialists such as doctors and teachers. A slave might hope to be given or to buy his freedom in which case he became a *libertus* (freedman).

Names

A Roman usually had three names: for example, Marcus Claudius Marcellus. Marcus (*praenomen*) is the name given at birth. Claudius (*nomen*) is the name of his family. Marcellus (*cognomen*) is a second name given at birth: it sometimes tells what branch of the family he belongs to. Roman women used the female form of their father's *nomen* — Claudia, plus a *cognomen* such as Prima. Slaves usually had only one name which was normally Greek. A freedman took the name of his former master and added his slave name as a *cognomen*.

The insulae

The whole town was split up into blocks (*insulae*). Each *insula* was walled and built up with houses, shops, restaurants and factories. Each building interlocked with the next like a jigsaw puzzle. This system probably evolved as circumstances changed and people sold off parts of their property either to the person next door or to commercial interests. The *insulae* varied in size from as little as 850 square metres to as large as 5,500 square metres. Some contained a dozen or more dwellings, others, such as region VI, *insula* 12, only one (the House of the Faun). Pompeii was not divided into rich and poor areas. Rich and poor seemed to live together in harmony. Many of the poorer houses are in the north-west corner of the town where there are also the two richest ones.

To give an idea of what an *insula* was like we have taken *insula* 6 in region I and reconstructed it. This block, which has an area of about 2,250 square metres, contains five houses complete with gardens, a laundry, a tavern, four shops, including an ironmonger's, and a bronzesmith's and also an underground bath house belonging to one of the houses. In the following pages these houses and shops are examined to try to see what life and conditions were like in a Roman town.

Right: A reconstruction of region I *insula* 6 as it was before the earthquake of AD 62. It is seen from the south.
1 The House of the Theatrical Paintings
2 The laundry of Stephanus
3 The house of Valerius Rufus
4 The garden of Valerius Rufus
5 The underground baths
6 A corner house with first-floor rented rooms at the front. The stairs up to these rooms can be seen to the right of the front door.
7 The house of L. Ceius Secundus
8 The house of Minucius the weaver

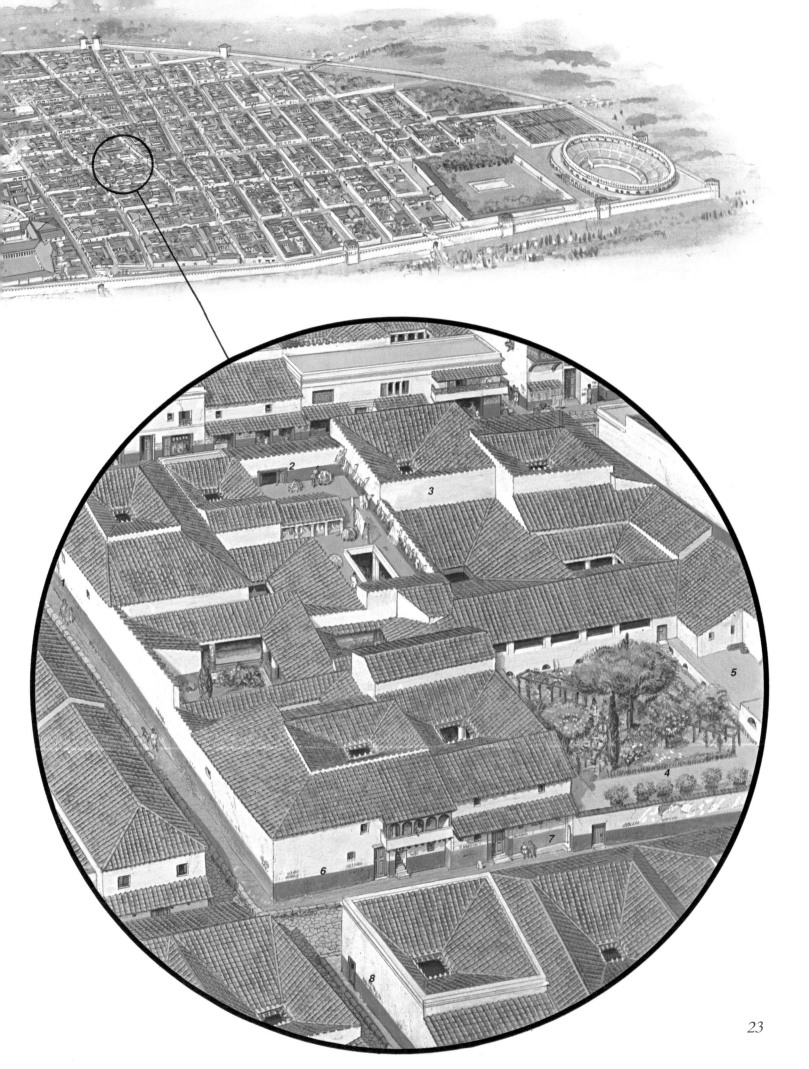

Inside the *insula*

A reconstruction

The picture on the right is a reconstruction of *insula* 6 in region I. Some of the roofing has been removed to show the inside. In the foreground is Pompeii's main east–west street known today as the via dell'Abbondanza. For the sake of clarity the *insula* will be described using the doorway numbers.

Region I *insula* 6

1 A shop of uncertain use with living quarters above. The front is shuttered but the side door is open.

2 The entrance to the house of Marcus Lucretius (also known as the House of the Cryptoporticus). To enter the house one passed down a passageway between two shops into the reception court (*atrium*), (*2a*). Beyond this is small garden, (*2b*). Four steps lead up to a summer dining room, (*2c*), which overlooked a large garden, (*2d*). From the small garden, (*2b*), another set of steps lead down to a crypt beneath the summer dining room. This crypt surrounded the small garden. It is about three metres below the ground level. Joined to the left side of the crypt is a bath house, (*2e*).

3 The shop of the bronzesmith Verus with living accommodation above it.

4 The entrance to the house of Valerius Rufus (or of the Trojan shrine). It was being decorated at the time of the eruption. The room at the back, (*4a*), was used as a workshop by the decorators. The bed shown on page 43, no. 7, was found in the bedroom, (*4b*). Before the earthquake nos. 2 and 4 were one large house.

5 A shop of uncertain use.

6 A stairway leading to a room above shop 5. This is one of many that were let out as bed-sitting rooms.

7 The entrance to the laundry and cloth-finishing establishment (*fullonica*) of Stephanus. At the back are large baths where the fabric was washed.

8 and 9 were being converted into a restaurant at the time of the eruption. 8 was a bar selling hot drinks. 9 was the entrance to the restaurant. Both belonged to the owner of house 11.

10 The shop of the ironmonger Junianus. This shop contained many tools and farm implements both new and secondhand. It had living quarters above.

11 The entrance to the House of the Theatrical Paintings, named after the paintings on the *atrium* walls.

12 This is a shop of uncertain use.

15 The house of Lucius Ceius Secundus. (This name is taken at random from the many names painted on the front of the house.) A full description of this house is given on the next page.

Region I *insula* 10

Insula 10 is at the top of the picture. In the centre is the famous House of the Menander. At the left end is a bar and tavern and at the right end is the house of the weaver Minucius.

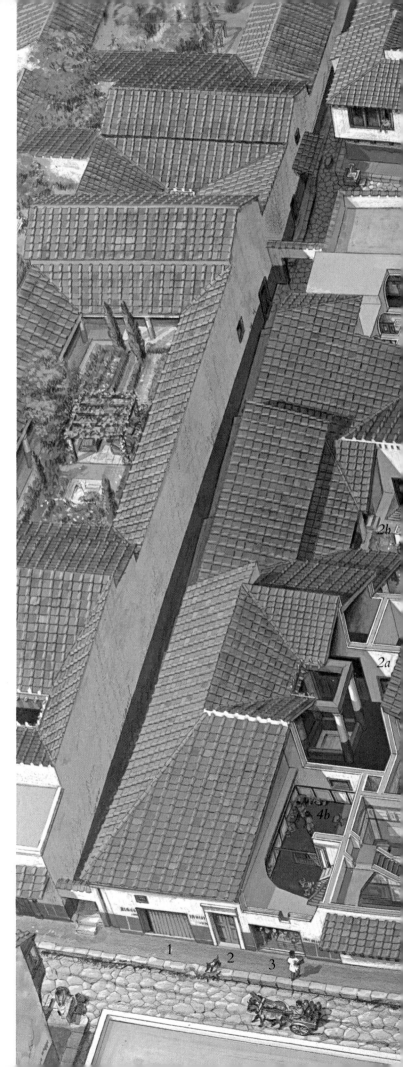

2d

2c

4a

15

4

5

6

7

8

9

10

11

12

Houses

The Italic house

The basic Italic house consisted of a courtyard surrounded by rooms with a small garden at the back (see right, no. 1). It was entered by a passageway (*fauces*) with a bedroom on either side. Often these two bedrooms were converted into shops which opened on to the street. The *fauces* led directly to the courtyard (*atrium*). This was roofed over except for a central hole through which rain fell into a basin set in the *atrium* floor. This rain water was collected in a well beneath the *atrium*.

Along each side of the *atrium* were bedrooms. The rear of the *atrium* was extended on either side to form two wings (*alae*). In the centre of the rear wall was a large room (*tablinum*). This was originally the master bedroom but later became the main reception room and office.

This type of house was later extended (no. 2) to include a colonnaded garden (peristyle). This often had fountains and an open-air dining room.

The Pompeian houses

It is very difficult to find houses at Pompeii that fit these basic designs. The difficulties of building within an *insula* forced architects to modify the plan. The house of Lucius Ceius Secundus in *insula* 6 is a good example of a modified Italic house (see top right). There was no room for bedrooms on either side of the *atrium*. These had to be put round the garden at the back of the house. There was also no room for the *tablinum* in the centre. It had to be moved to the left. Bedrooms were built on either side of the entrance but later the one to the left of the entrance was turned into a kitchen. The ceiling was lowered and servants' quarters were built above it.

Just before the eruption of Vesuvius it was decided that the house was still too small. A stairway was put in leading up to a balcony built along the rear wall of the *atrium*. From here a corridor, constructed above the passageway to the garden, led to upstairs bedrooms at the back of the house. These alterations were not complete at the time of the eruption: the boxed-in stairway had not yet been plastered.

The rich and the poor

As the taste for luxury increased so the houses of the rich grew. No. 5 at the bottom is the vast House of the Faun with its two *atria* and two peristyles. The life of the poor was not quite so luxurious. Around Pompeii one can see many of the little rooms occupied by the poor (see no. 4). These are built into the fronts of houses at first-floor level. A stairway leads up from the street level. If there was more than one room a balcony was built along the front of the house to give access to the rooms.

Right: A reconstruction of the house of L. Ceius Secundus (region I, *insula* 6, no. 15). The house is entered up a sloping passageway. On the left of the passageway is the kitchen (the wall has been cut away to show it). The servants' quarters are above. The roof of the *atrium* is supported by four columns. Behind these columns is the boxed-in stairway with a cupboard underneath. The *tablinum* is at the far side of the back of the *atrium*. At the rear of the house is a small garden with a scene of wild animals hunting painted on the wall. Other rooms: *C* bedrooms, *D* dining room.

Below: The front of the house of L. Ceius Secundus.

1 The Italic house with its central *atrium* and rooms grouped around it.
2 The later Italic house with a peristyle attached.
A *Atrium*
C Bedroom (*cubiculum*)
H Garden (*hortus*)
P Peristyle
T *Tablinum*
X Wing (*ala*)
3 The house of a shopkeeper
S Shop
4 Bed-sitting rooms built into the front of a house. A stairway leads up from the pavement. Individual rooms can be reached from a balcony running along the front of the house.

5 The vast House of the Faun (region VI, *insula* 12). It has two *atria* and two peristyles. The front bedrooms have been turned into shops.

Construction and decoration

Building materials and construction techniques

The main building materials were limestone, *tufa* (which consists of volcanic ash hardened into stone by the action of water) and brick, which was mainly used for corners of buildings and door posts.

Before 200 BC houses were built of rubble bonded with clay and held together by a limestone framework (see right *1*). The fronts of these houses were built of large rectangular blocks of limestone (*2*).

After 200 BC new techniques were gradually introduced. The most common was a mixture of rubble and cement called *opus incertum* or *opus caementicium* (*3*).

Opus reticulatum (*4*) was made from small square blocks of stone laid in diagonal lines giving the appearance of network (*reticulum*) from which it gets its name. This formed only the surface of the wall. The inside was rubble and cement. *Quasi reticulatum* is a cruder form of (*4*).

Opus mixtum — alternating courses of brick and stone (*5*) — was often used to make corners. *Opus craticium* (*6*), which consisted of a light wood frame filled with rubble and plaster, was used for building partitions and balconies.

Roofs and windows

Roofs were covered with rectangular tiles (*tegulae*) about 45 by 60cm. The junction between two tiles was covered by a semi-cylindrical tile (*imbrex*).

Windows were often just a slit in the outside wall widened on the inside to let in maximum light. They were sometimes glazed. Larger windows were often barred with an iron grille and sometimes shuttered.

1 The earliest house-building technique found at Pompeii. Rubble masonry held in place by a limestone frame.

4 Opus reticulatum made from small square stones laid in diagonal lines. The less regular form is called *quasi reticulatum.*

6 Opus craticium: a timber framework filled with rubble and plaster.

2 Rectangular blocks used for the front of houses.

3 Opus incertum: masonry made from rubble and cement.

5 Opus mixtum: alternating courses of bricks and stone, usually two or three of brick to one of stone.

7 Terracotta drainage pipes set into the wall of a house.

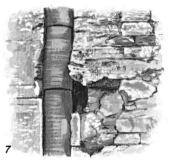

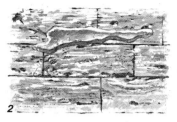

12 A window with an iron grille.
13 A terracotta window grille.
14 A slit window from the inside.
15 A porthole-type window from the inside.

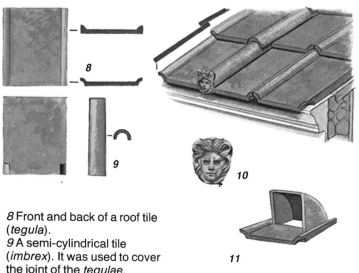

8 Front and back of a roof tile (*tegula*).
9 A semi-cylindrical tile (*imbrex*). It was used to cover the joint of the *tegulae.*
10 An *antefix*. It was used to cover the end of the *imbrex.*
11 A window tile used to let in light.

Wall decoration

The development of Pompeian decoration is very complex. Only some general trends can be shown here. The decorations have been split up into four historical groups known as the four styles.

The first, or masonry style, which lasted until about 80 BC, imitated slabs of coloured marble. The second, or architectural style added architectural motifs and landscapes to give an illusion of depth.

The third style, which developed towards the end of the first century BC, did away with the illusion of space but kept a sort of fantasy architecture which was often used to frame a picture.

The fourth style came in about the middle of the first century AD. It is a very varied style. Where it is a continuation of the third style the pictures get smaller or disappear and the architectural forms become more wiry and lack solidity.

Right: The early third style. The example comes from the Villa of Poppaea at Torre Annunziata. The search for depth has been abandoned. The columns, so characteristic of the second style, still appear but in an elongated form. Often, as here, they are used to frame a picture. Another characteristic is the use of a large flat panels of colour.

Left: The fully developed second style. The example comes from the Villa of Poppaea at Torre Annunziata. The illusion of depth has been achieved. The use of buildings and trees in the background, plus tripods, gates and animals at various depths in the middle ground all help to create the illusion than the columns are in front of the rest of the wall.

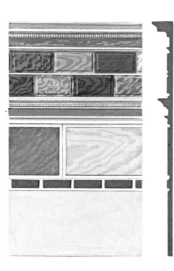

Left: The first or masonry style. The example comes from a bedroom (region VI, *insula* 9, no. 5). The shape of the imitation marble blocks and the cornices is modelled in a type of plaster called stucco.

Left: The developed third style. The example comes from the dining room of L. Ceius Secundus (region I, *insula* 6, no. 15). Here the large black panels and long blocks of red concentrate the eye on the picture in the centre. The columns and the architrave, which runs along the top of the panels in the previous styles, have been modified to become a white frame for the picture and a narrow panel along the top. The light panel above with its architectural designs is a characteristic of the third and fourth style.

Right: The late first style. The example comes from the temple of Jupiter in the Forum. The imitation slabs of marble are seldom moulded, the three-dimensional effect is achieved by the use of light and shade. Narrow upright blocks have been introduced and panels are often framed.

Right: An example of the fourth style. It comes from the house of Octavius Quartio (region II, *insula* 2, no. 2). This is only one example of the variety of different designs that make up the fourth style. It has been chosen because it shows a direct development from the third style. The columns of the earlier period have been replaced by tall wiry architectural forms. The picture in the middle has been reduced to just a tiny figure. Along the top are more fantasy buildings joined by garlands.

Left: The early second style. The example comes from the Villa of the Mysteries outside Pompeii. Many of the elements of the first style have been kept, but columns standing on a plinth create the illusion that the panels between the columns are set back. The illusion is further enhanced by the coffered arches at the top.

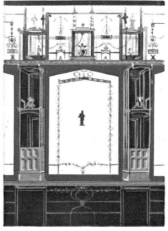

The entrance

The facade

The walls of Pompeian houses were plastered over and painted both inside and out. Outside walls were painted white. Along the bottom they usually had a coloured panel about two metres high. This was normally painted red. On the outside walls, especially near doorways, one finds slogans lettered in red and black. These include such things as advertisements and election slogans 'All the fruit sellers with Helvius Vestalis support the election of M. Holconius Priscus as *duumvir*.' The high standard of the lettering leaves no doubt that there was a special body of professional signwriters employed to put up these posters. There were also innumerable graffiti: 'Do not relieve yourself here — the stinging nettles are long'.

The doorway

The entrance, which was in the form of a passage (*fauces*), led straight into the *atrium*. In older houses it was often divided in two. The part nearest the street (*vestibulum*) was where guests removed their cloaks before passing through the front door.

Door posts were often decorated in the form of two columns supporting an architrave. In the later houses the doors were usually pivoted just behind these artificial columns. The Romans disliked single-leaf doors and wherever possible, both inside and out, they used double or even folding doors. No doors have survived but several have left their imprint in the ashes and casts have been made using Fiorelli's process. On some of these doors the locking system can still be seen. On others great bronze studs have survived in position. Many door knockers and handles have been found and are now in the museum at Naples.

The floor of the entrance to a wealthy house is often decorated with mosaics. Wild animals, such as boars, are a popular motif. In the entrance of one house is a mosaic showing a chained dog baring its teeth with the warning '*Cave canem*' —beware of the dog.

The thief in the night

Pompeii had no real police force. The inhabitants went to great lengths to protect themselves and their property. This is one of the reasons that one finds so few windows at street level. Those there are, are usually either slit windows or are closed with an iron grille. At night doors were locked and barred. One door which was cast by Fiorelli's process was not only barred but it also had a long prop jammed against it so that it could not be broken down (see far right at top). Often a hole to stop the bar sliding can be seen in the floor of the *fauces*.

Many keys have been found. These and pieces of locks have been used to make the reconstruction on the right.

Above: The entrance to the house of L. Ceius Secundus. This is one of the very few examples where the ceiling has survived.
Right: The entrance to an older Pompeian house. Note the false pillars and architrave. Cloaks were removed in the *vestibulum* (*A*) before going through the door and passing down the *fauces* (*B*). At the end is the *atrium* and *tablinum*.
Below: A mosaic in the entrance of a house showing a chained dog with bared teeth. Underneath is written '*Cave canem*' — beware of the dog.

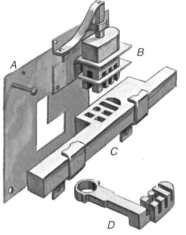

Above: A plaster cast of a door with bar and prop.
Left: Reconstruction of a lock. The lock plate *A* is riveted to the outside of the door. The lock *B* and the bolt *C* are fixed to the inside of the door. The bolt is slid along until the teeth of the lock slip down into the holes in the bolt. It is now locked. To unlock it the key *D* is inserted through the L-shaped hole and used to push the lock up out of the holes in the bolt. The bolt can be drawn back with the key.

Above: Doorway to a house with its doors cast in plaster (region II, *insula* 5, no. 4).

Left: A painting from Boscoreale showing a highly decorated entrance to a house.

Right: The *vestibulum* of the House of the Faun elaborately decorated in the first style.

Below and right: Plaster casts of doors. One shows the traces of the locks and the other has large bronze studs.

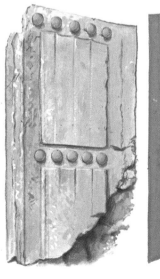

The reception rooms 1: the *atrium*

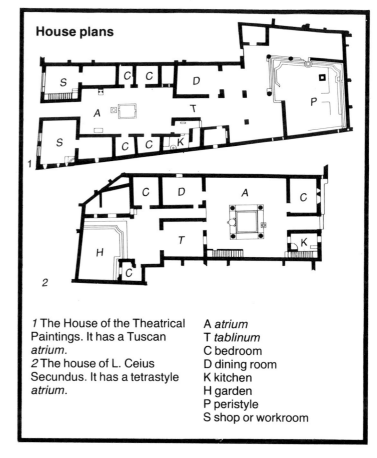

House plans

1 The House of the Theatrical Paintings. It has a Tuscan *atrium*.
2 The house of L. Ceius Secundus. It has a tetrastyle *atrium*.

A *atrium*
T *tablinum*
C bedroom
D dining room
K kitchen
H garden
P peristyle
S shop or workroom

The *compluvium* and *impluvium*

Passing along the *fauces* one enters the *atrium*. Here the family received guests. The *atrium* was normally covered by a roof which sloped inwards. The rain water ran down towards the centre where there was a large rectangular hole (*compluvium*). Here it passed through spouts in the shape of animals, such as dogs, wolves and lions, and fell into a large rectangular basin (*impluvium*) set into the floor of the *atrium*. Originally the water drained into a shaft which carried it down to a cistern. Here it was kept for use in the household. The cistern shaft was capped with a cylinder of stone or terracotta probably to prevent young children falling in. After the construction of the aqueduct most houses were supplied with running water and no longer needed to store rain water.

The *atrium* roof was supported by two massive timber beams. The roof structure is best understood by looking at the diagram on the right. An *atrium* roofed in this way is known as a Tuscan *atrium*. The vast majority of Pompeian *atria* are of this type. Two of the seven *atria* in *insula* 6 (nos. 2 and 15) have roofs supported by four columns. These are called tetrastyle *atria*. A third type, which is very rare at Pompeii, is the Corinthian *atrium*. Here the roof is supported by six or more columns.

The *atrium* of the theatrical paintings

As has been said (p.26) the traditional *atrium* had bedrooms on either side, wings (*alae*) at the end and a large room (*tablinum*) in the centre of the rear wall. None of the seven *atria* in *insula* 6 fits this description. (The tavern (8/9) and the laundry (7), are included in this number as both are converted houses.) The nearest is the *atrium* of the theatrical paintings (no. 11). This has bedrooms and *tablinum* in the right place but no wings (see right).

This *atrium* is decorated simply in the later third style with small paintings of theatrical scenes set into large blue panels. The doorways on the left lead to bedrooms. They are matched by two bedrooms on the right. The broad opening with the lattice-work screen is the *tablinum*. The small door on the right leads to the kitchen and garden. In the corner stands a small wooden altar in the form of a temple. This is the *lararium,* the shrine of the household gods. On the left is a strong box. Neither of these was found in this house but they are commonly found in the *atrium*.

At the far end of the *impluvium*, which is decorated with coloured marble, is a white marble table. This table, with each leg carved in the form of a lion's head and back legs, is of great historical interest for on it is carved the name P. Casca Longus — one of the conspirators who assassinated Caesar. His property was confiscated. Could this have belonged to him?

Right: A reconstruction of the *atrium* of the theatrical paintings.

Above: The shrine of the household gods *(lararium)* from the House of the Vettii (region VI, *insula* 15). The head of the household offered prayers and gifts to these gods daily.

Above: The *impluvium* in the *atrium* of the theatrical paintings.

Above: The *compluvium* of the house of Valerius Rufus (region I, *insula* 6, no. 4). One can see the rainwater spouts shaped like wolves and a lion.

1 A section of an *impluvium* showing the shaft going down to the cistern and the cylinder capping the shaft.
2 A marble cylinder for capping the shaft.
3 An elaborately carved marble table. One or more tables usually stood at the end of the *impluvium*. They could also be made of bronze or wood.

The roof of a Tuscan *atrium*

1 A plan view of the roof of a Tuscan *atrium*. Some of the tiles have been removed to show the position of the beams and rafters.
2 A section of the same roof.
3 Reconstructed rainwater spouts from a *compluvium*.
4 A section of a compluviate roof and rainwater spout.

The reception rooms 2: the *tablinum*

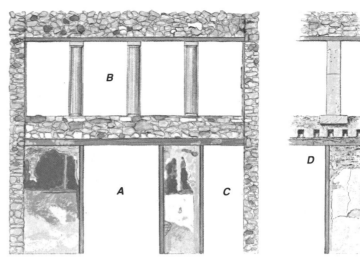

The dawn callers

Callers began to gather outside the houses of the wealthy even before daybreak. If the house had a *vestibulum* they would wait here for the doors to open. If not they had to wait in the street whatever the weather. Some houses, such as the house of Ceius (no. 15 in *insula* 6), and the Samnite House at Herculaneum (right) had stone benches at the front where callers could wait. These dawn callers were the dependants (*clientes*) of the master of the house (*patron*). *Clientes* received financial and other support from their *patron*. He, in return, would receive their support in his political or business ventures. The tie between *clientes* and *patron* was strong. Neither could be forced to bear witness against the other in the law courts.

There were three types of *clientes*: poor freeborn citizens who had placed themselves under the protection of the master of the house; freedmen who owed their liberty to him, and hangers-on hoping for a handout (*sportula*). These hangers-on might attach themselves to more than one household. They would go from one house to another early each morning to see how much they could collect.

At six o'clock the doors of the house opened and the callers would be ushered into the *atrium*. Here they waited until their *patron* was ready to receive them. A slave announced them and showed them into the *tablinum* where the master received them one at a time.

The reception of the *clientes* lasted until eight o'clock. Some callers might be asked to wait and accompany the patron as he went about his business.

The *tablinum*

The *tablinum* was at the back of the *atrium*. It had originally been the main bedroom. Later it became the record room where the family documents were kept. It was often completely open at the front divided from the *atrium* only by curtains or wooden screens. Some of these have been found at Herculaneum (see box above right). Even where there was a door there was usually a large window as well. This was probably so that the owner could see who the callers were and if necessary refuse to receive them.

The *tablinum* often opened directly on to the garden. This is so with three of the houses in *insula* 6, (nos. 11, 13 and 15). The other two (nos. 2 and 4) have large windows at the back. These openings could be closed with folding doors. Just such doors have been found in the Villa of Poppaea at Torre Annunziata.

One building in *insula* 6, the house that was being converted into a tavern (no. 8/9), had a room above the *tablinum* with a colonnaded front overlooking the *atrium*. There are only a few examples of these. The best is the Samnite House at Herculaneum (see right).

Left: The facade of the *tablinum* of the house that was being converted into a tavern (region I, *insula* 6, no. 8/9). The *tablinum* (A) has an open front. Above it is the colonnaded loggia (*B*). The doorway (*C*) led to the stairs. At the back of the facade (*D*) the holes for the rafters that supported the upper floor can be seen.

Below: A reconstruction of the Samnite House at Herculaneum. Its *tablinum* has a door and large window. Above it is the colonnaded loggia.

Wooden screens

1 Lattice shutters
2 A wooden partition with double doors at either end. The centre panels have been restored.
3 A retractable lattice screen.
3a A detail of the same screen. Such wooden objects were preserved in the mud at Herculaneum.

1

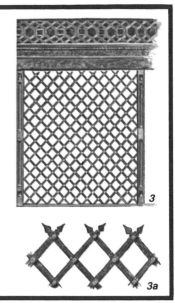

3

3a

2

The kitchen and toilet

The kitchen

The Pompeians loved good food. Cooks were valued members of the household. A good one could be expensive. As cooks were usually slaves the kitchen itself was considered unimportant. There is no set place for the kitchen in a Pompeian house. It is usually found somewhere behind the *atrium*.

The kitchen in the house of Ceius is on the left of the entrance. It had probably been at the back of the house and was moved when bedrooms were built around the garden. Being a small house the Ceius family would have had only two or three servants. They converted one of the front bedrooms into a kitchen and servants' quarters. The floor of the bedroom was lowered and the roof raised to make space for attic rooms above the kitchen. A stairway was put in at the side of the kitchen to give access to these attic rooms.

Upper floors were usually made by inserting rafters with planks laid across them. A compound of brick chips and mortar (about 10cm thick) was laid over the planks to make a durable surface. There are many examples of this at Herculaneum.

Kitchen equipment

Kitchens usually consisted of little more than an oven and a sink. The oven was built of bricks with a flat surface where the fire was kindled above an arch where fuel was stored. Food was either boiled in pots held above the flames on a small tripod or grilled on a gridiron. There was no chimney. The smoke drifted away through the window.

A kitchen was discovered when the laundry of Stephanus (*insula* 6, no. 7) was excavated. Lunch was being prepared for the staff when the eruption came. The cook fled leaving a pot still on the boil. Other cooking utensils were found hanging on the wall or resting on the side of the oven ready for use.

Innumerable pots and pans have been found at Pompeii. They are made either of earthenware or bronze. Bronze pots often have bucket-type handles. Ladles and strainers have also been found.

The strange apparatus in the corner (bottom right) is a portable heater for liquids. Liquid was kept in the large cylinder (*A*). From here it flowed around the semi-circular part (*B*) where charcoal was burned. It was heated here and drawn off by the tap (*C*). The box was for storing the fuel. The Romans liked their wine hot. This apparatus was probably a wine heater.

Toilets

The Pompeians had little appreciation of hygiene. Open toilets are usually found either next to, or, as in the house of Ceius, actually in the kitchen. They usually drained away into a pit. Only public toilets had a proper sewage system.

Above: A shop at Herculaneum showing wooden stairs and the construction of the upper floor – rafters with planks laid across them. A surface, usually a mixture of brick chips in mortar, was laid over the planking.

Above: A reconstruction of the kitchen in the house of Ceius. The wall has been cut away to show the toilet which is under the stairs.

Left: The kitchen in the laundry of Stephanus with all the pots and pans as they were found.

Right: A portable liquid heater.
A The cylinder with a hinged lid where the liquid was kept.
B The heater where a charcoal fire was burned.
C The tap.

Kitchen utensils

1, 2, 3 Bronze pans
No *1* has a bucket-type handle and rests on an iron tripod.
4 Grid iron
5 Earthenware jug
6 Bronze ladle
7 Bronze strainer
8 Earthenware pot with lid
9 Earthenware strainer

The dining room

Winter dining rooms

The dining room in a Pompeian house is probably the most interesting room because it was so different from our own. Romans reclined on couches leaning on their left elbows and eating with their right hands. The arrangement of a Roman dining room was very formal. It consisted of three large sloping couches covered with cushions. These couches, which sloped backwards, were placed on three sides of the table. It was these three couches which gave the dining room its name (*triclinium*).

In Pompeii, dining rooms were often very small. Niches had to be cut in the walls to make room for the wooden couches. From this we know their size — 4.5 by 9 Roman feet (1.3 by 2.6 metres). Each couch held three people who reclined at an angle across it (see diagram on right). The places were fixed by custom. The master of the house would occupy the first place (*A*) on the left-hand couch. Next to him, on the same couch, would be his wife and at the end his son or freedman. Next to the master of the house but on the middle couch was the chief guest (*B*). The other guests occupied the remaining places.

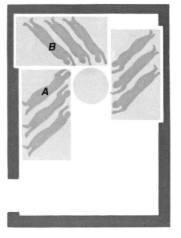

Above: The summer *triclinium* built over the *cryptoporticus* at the back of the house of M. Lucretius (region I, *insula* 6, no. 2).
Left: The plan of a winter *triclinium* with niches cut into the walls to take the couches.
A The master of the house
B The chief guest
Below: A painting probably showing the end of a banquet. The table has been removed and the guests are drinking. The man on the right is drunk and being supported by a slave.

Summer dining rooms

The dining room described above was for winter use. During the summer it was more pleasant to dine in the garden or in a room opening on to the garden. Many *triclinia* of this sort have been found. These dining areas usually have couches in the form of a three-sided square (see right above). This example is from the house of Lucretius (no. 2 in *insula* 6). On the left-hand side of the room broad windows open on to the garden. The couches were generally of masonry so that they would not rot in the wet winter months.

There was a third type of dining room called a *cenaculum.* It was upstairs. This is probably the function of the colonnaded rooms built over the *tablinum* (see p.34).

Food and tableware

Several *triclinia* have been found with lunch already laid on the table. At one house in Herculaneum bread, salad, eggs, cake and fruit were found on the table preserved by the sea of mud that engulfed the town. The shells of the eggs were not even broken. These are only some of the many types of food that have either been found or are represented on wall paintings. As it was a seaside town it is not surprising that sea food was popular. Fish of many kinds, octopus and lobster are shown on the wall paintings. The paintings also show poultry, rabbits and various fruits and vegetables, including mushrooms. A large quantity of tableware has been found. This was mainly bronze. Drinking vessels of bronze, silver and coloured glass have also been discovered.

Below: A table laid ready for lunch in the house of Arrius Crescens (region III, *insula* 4, nos. 2-3).

Above: A summer dining room at the back of the house of Octavius Quartio (region II, *insula* 2, no. 2). This is unique as it has only two couches and should be called a *biclinium*.

Tableware

Left: 1, 2, 3 Coloured glassware. Jugs of almost identical design are also found in bronze and silver.
4 Silver egg-cup
5 Silver two-handled cup
6 Bronze pan (*patera*)
7 Silver plate
8 Bronze spoons
9 Bronze dish

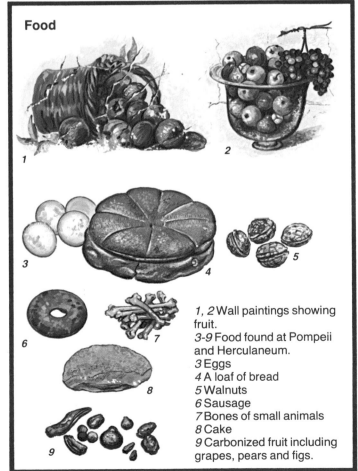

Food

1, 2 Wall paintings showing fruit.
3-9 Food found at Pompeii and Herculaneum.
3 Eggs
4 A loaf of bread
5 Walnuts
6 Sausage
7 Bones of small animals
8 Cake
9 Carbonized fruit including grapes, pears and figs.

Dinner parties

A code of behaviour

Most Pompeian dining rooms were very small and had only just room for the three couches and table.

Although wall paintings often show servants behind the diners usually it would only have been possible to serve from the open end of the room. The very system of reclining in cramped conditions where one person 'lay on the breast' of the next meant that a strict code of behaviour had to be observed. Wine flowed freely and parties often got very bawdy. This prompted one Pompeian to have rules of behaviour printed on the wall of his dining room:

'A slave must wash and dry the feet of the guests – and let him be sure to spread a linen cloth over the cushions on the couches.

Don't cast lustful glances or make eyes at another man's wife.

Don't be coarse in your conversation.

Restrain yourself from getting angry or using offensive language. If you can't, then go back to your own house.'

The banquet of Trimalchio

The main meal (cena) was eaten in the evening. It normally consisted of three courses. The Roman writer Petronius, in his extravagant and farcical novel *The Satyricon*, tells of a banquet at the house of Trimalchio, a vastly wealthy freedman. The story is set in the Naples area shortly before the eruption. The description is exaggerated but it gives us some idea of the sort of meal that might be served in a wealthy Pompeian house. The dinner consisted of eight courses. This is the menu:

1 Dormice in honey, sprinkled with poppy seeds, hot sausages, damsons, olives and pomegranate seeds.

2 Hare served with sow's udders.

3 A female wild boar with a small basket hung from each tusk – one contained fresh and the other dried dates. The boar was laid on its side and piglets made of marzipan were arranged as if they were feeding.

4 A large pig stuffed with sausages and blood puddings.

5 A boiled calf.

6 A fat chicken and goose eggs served to each guest.

7 Thrushes rolled in flour and stuffed with nuts and raisins. This was followed by quinces stuck with prickles to look like sea urchins.

8 A dish made up to look like a goose surrounded by fish and birds of various kinds. It was in fact made completely from parts of a pig.

This whole meal was served up with delicacies between the courses and a plentiful supply of wine. After the meal the remains were given to the servants.

A dinner party in the house of Lucius Ceius Secundus.

The bedrooms

Bedrooms

In the traditional Italic house the bedrooms were grouped around the *atrium*. As has been shown the plan of most Pompeian houses had to be modified to fit the available area. In *insula* 6 only one *atrium* (no. 11) has bedrooms on both sides. The plan was modified further when the front bedrooms were converted into shops. Along the north side of *insula* 6 only house no. 4 has kept its front bedrooms.

Bedrooms seldom had windows. Even the front bedrooms of no. 4 have none. Occasionally they had small slit windows opening on to the *atrium*. However, on the south side of *insula* 6 the front bedrooms of no. 13 and the house of Ceius next door, have windows opening on to the street. The bedroom in the house of Ceius (no. 15) is exceptional, having both a slit window and a wider rectangular window.

Beds

Only the metal parts of beds, such as the legs have been found at Pompeii. Two beds found in the House of the Menander have been reconstructed from their bronze fittings. A further two beds were cast by Fiorelli's process from imprints left in the house of Valerius Rufus (no. 4 in *insula* 6).

It has been assumed that the centre of the bed was strung to allow some give beneath the mattress. However several complete beds were preserved in the mud at Herculaneum (see (5) in the box on the right). These have a wooden grid across the centre.

Mattresses, pillows and other bed clothes are often shown on wall paintings. These are usually striped.

Toiletries

A large number of toilet accessories have been recovered from Pompeii and Herculaneum. Among these are bone and ivory combs and hair pins. The ivory hairpin (5) is decorated with a little carving of Pudicitia, the personification of modesty and chastity. Several pins have this motif, which seems to belie the belief that Pompeian women were shameless and immoral. There are also bronze and silver mirrors polished on the front and often decorated on the back. Ivory and glass cosmetic jars have also been found.

Jewellery

Many pieces of jewellery have come to light. These include rings, bracelets, armbands, necklaces, pendants, amulets and earrings. Roman jewellery was generally appreciated for its size rather than its quality: the women in *The Satyricon* boast of the weight, not the beauty, of their jewellery. The gold bulla (9) was found in the House of the Menander. The bulla was the symbol of free birth and was worn by boys from infancy until manhood.

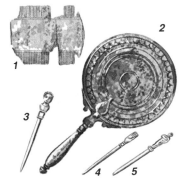

3, 4, 5 Ivory hair pins with decorated tops.

6 Front of a bronze table mirror. The disc would be highly polished to produce a reflection.
7 An ivory pin jar
8 An ivory cosmetic jar

Cosmetic articles

1 A double-sided bone hair comb. This is the normal shape of ancient combs.
2 The back of a silver hand mirror.

Above: A reconstruction of the front bedroom of the house of Ceius.

12 A cluster earring made of gold, pearls and green plasma.
13 Flexible gold bracelet.
14 An earthenware chamber pot found under a bed at Herculaneum.

Jewellery
9 A gold bulla
10 A gold ring in the form of a coiled snake.
11 A gold armband also in the form of a coiled snake.

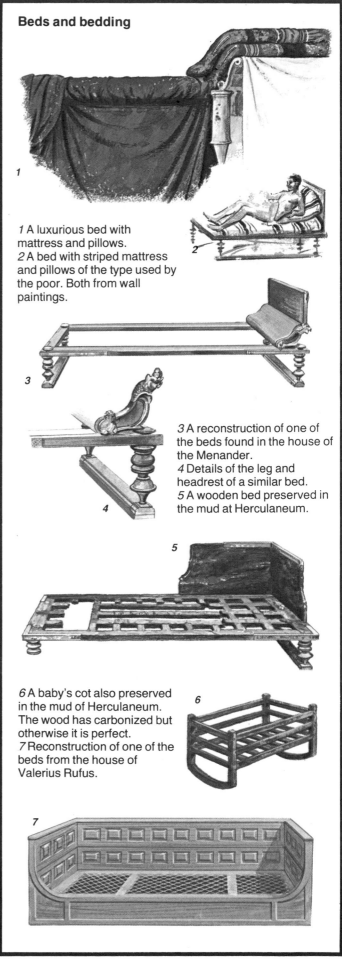

Beds and bedding

1 A luxurious bed with mattress and pillows.
2 A bed with striped mattress and pillows of the type used by the poor. Both from wall paintings.

3 A reconstruction of one of the beds found in the house of the Menander.
4 Details of the leg and headrest of a similar bed.
5 A wooden bed preserved in the mud at Herculaneum.

6 A baby's cot also preserved in the mud of Herculaneum. The wood has carbonized but otherwise it is perfect.
7 Reconstruction of one of the beds from the house of Valerius Rufus.

Furniture, lighting and heating

Furniture found at Pompeii

The Romans did not use as much furniture as we do. Some articles, such as tables and chairs, were probably moved around as they were needed. Wooden furniture has not survived at Pompeii except in the form of plaster casts made from imprints in the ashes. However a large number of stone and bronze pieces have been found. These are mainly tables and benches.

Wooden furniture from Herculaneum

The situation at Herculaneum is very different. The sea of boiling mud rolled down the hillside seeping under doors and through windows. It completely filled the houses preserving everything within them. It charred the wood turning it to carbon. The wood has survived through the ages in this form.

Most of the people of Herculaneum fled when the eruption started. Only a few were caught. The mud, oozing down the hillside, filled the stream beds first: once it had engulfed the bridges there was no escape. One boy who was too ill to flee was found still lying on his bed which, being wood, was preserved in the mud.

What was a tragedy for Herculaneum was a godsend for the archaeologist. Tables, couches, cupboards, beds and other wooden bits and pieces were preserved in the mud as were various types of food and fabrics such as rope, fishing nets and shoes.

Two of the best-preserved pieces from Herculaneum are the wood and leather couch (7) and the altar to the household gods (12). The altar is shaped like a temple whose folding doors make a cupboard for the vessels needed for the daily service.

Lighting and heating

Indoor lighting was provided by candles or oil lamps. Literally thousands of lamps have been found – 1,328 were found in the Forum baths alone. These lamps were made of terracotta or bronze (see 1–4 in the box). Oil was poured in through a hole in the centre which was closed with a plug. On metal lamps the plug was often attached to the handle by a chain (see 2).

The lamps had one or more spouts with wicks in them. The oil soaked up the wick providing a constant supply of fuel to the flame. These lamps only gave off a small amount of light. A large number were required to light a room. Many lamp stands have been found. Most were made to support only one lamp but some held as many as fourteen. Some (see 7) have an adjustable height so that they can be used for reading.

Lanterns or torches were used outside. Lanterns (see 5/5a) were usually made of bronze with transparent sides of horn or bladder. They were illuminated by a candle made of tallow fat around a twisted wick.

In the cold days of winter, heating was provided by small charcoal-burning braziers made of bronze.

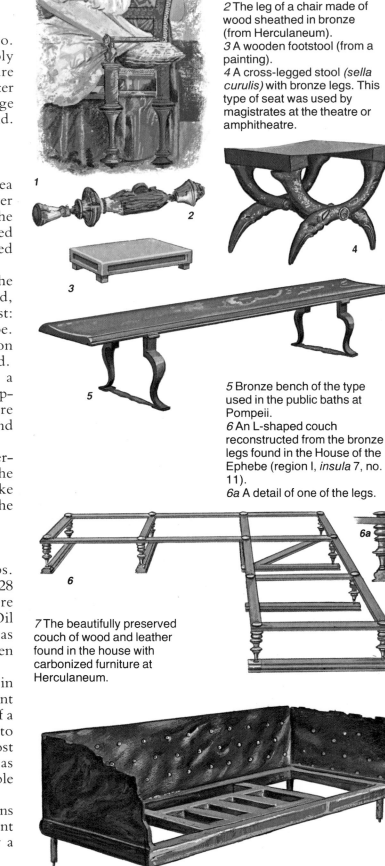

1 A wall painting from a villa at Boscoreale on the slopes of Vesuvius showing a painted wooden armchair.
2 The leg of a chair made of wood sheathed in bronze (from Herculaneum).
3 A wooden footstool (from a painting).
4 A cross-legged stool (sella curulis) with bronze legs. This type of seat was used by magistrates at the theatre or amphitheatre.

5 Bronze bench of the type used in the public baths at Pompeii.
6 An L-shaped couch reconstructed from the bronze legs found in the House of the Ephebe (region I, insula 7, no. 11).
6a A detail of one of the legs.

7 The beautifully preserved couch of wood and leather found in the house with carbonized furniture at Herculaneum.

8 A bronze table with marble top from the house of Cuspius Pansa (region I, *insula* 7, no. 1).
9 A wooden table with carved legs from Herculaneum. These three-legged tables were exceedingly popular.
10 A bronze and marble table from the House of the Menander.

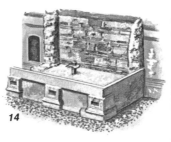

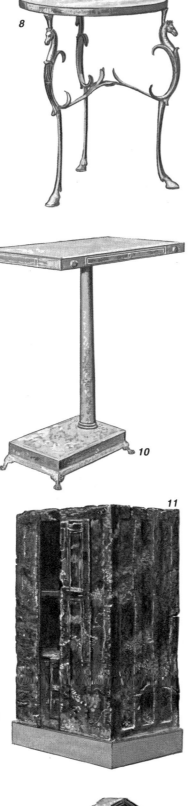

14 The base of a strong box in the *atrium* of the House of the Vettii (region VI, *insula* 12). In the middle is the iron bar which riveted the box to the floor.

15 An iron and bronze strongbox in which the household valuables were kept. The strongbox was usually found in the *atrium*.

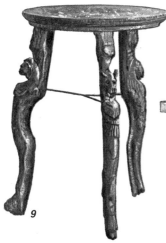

11 A wooden cupboard with shelves and hinged doors.
12 A wooden shrine of the household gods *(lararium).* It is in the form of a miniature temple. Underneath is a cupboard for the sacred vessels.
13 Part of a similar *lararium* showing the top which is missing on *12.*
11-13 are from Herculaneum.

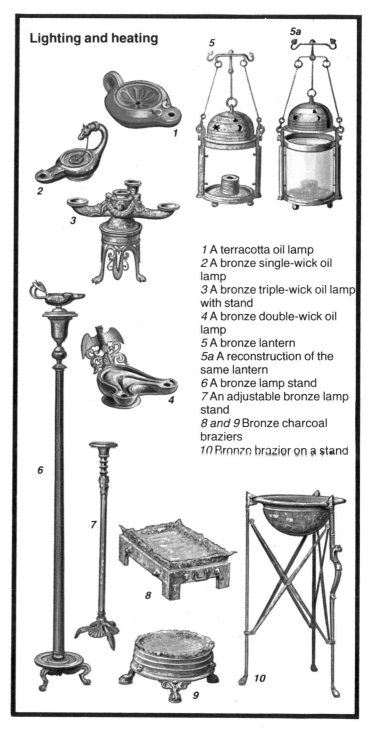

Lighting and heating

1 A terracotta oil lamp
2 A bronze single-wick oil lamp
3 A bronze triple-wick oil lamp with stand
4 A bronze double-wick oil lamp
5 A bronze lantern
5a A reconstruction of the same lantern
6 A bronze lamp stand
7 An adjustable bronze lamp stand
8 and 9 Bronze charcoal braziers
10 Bronze brazier on a stand

The garden

Small gardens and peristyles

Very few gardens in Pompeii have been properly examined. Archaeologists have only recently really started looking at gardens. It is becoming clear that all houses had gardens. Many areas within houses which were once thought to be rooms with missing floors are now being re-examined to see if they were gardens.

The walls that surround small gardens were often painted with outdoor scenes in an attempt to make the garden seem larger. The garden of Ceius with its hunting scenes is a good example.

The most popular type of garden was undoubtedly the peristyle with its colonnades where one could walk in the shade during the heat of the day. Ideally this type of garden had colonnades on all four sides. There are many examples of these, such as the House of the Menander, but there are others where the colonnade is on two or three sides only. Three of the houses in *insula* 6 (2, 8/9 and 11) have peristyles with colonnades on only two sides. Marble discs (*oscilla*) were often hung between the columns. These would revolve in the breeze flashing as they caught the sun.

The best preserved peristyle in Pompeii is in the House of the Vettii. It is adorned with statues and fountains. The excavators have replanted the garden and tried to restore it to its former beauty.

The garden of Octavius Quartio

The most remarkable garden at Pompeii is that belonging to Octavius Quartio. This garden occupies nearly two-thirds of the whole insula. The garden was divided in two by a canal which was fed by a fountain at the far end of the garden. On either side of the canal were trellised avenues. As the canal approached the house it passed beneath a pergola and joined a long pond which ran along the terrace at the back of the house. At the east end of this was the summer dining room shown on page 39. Casts were made of the root cavities in the garden and from these it was possible to determine what type of trees and bushes grew there.

The two gardens just described were carefully planted to a plan. This may not have been the rule. A garden has recently been discovered where trees were not planted in a regular pattern.

Vineyards and orchards

The archaeologist leading this new examination of gardens is an American, Wilhelmina Jashemsky. In the last few years, besides her work on private gardens, she has excavated a market garden, an orchard and a vineyard within the walls of Pompeii. During her excavation of the vineyard she found the root holes of fifty-eight trees and around 2,000 vines each with a stake to support it. The vineyard was laid out on a rectangular grid with four Roman feet between plants.

Above: The painted walls of the garden of Ceius (region I, *insula* 6, no. 15).
Right above: The garden of the Vettii (region VI, *insula* 15, no. 1).
Right below: The garden of Octavius Quartio seen from the terrace. The canal can be seen in the centre (region II, *insula* 2, no. 2).
Below: A reconstruction of the garden of Octavius Quartio.

Above: A plaster cast of a tree root.

Left: A white marble *oscillum*. These were often hung between the columns of the peristyle.

46

Private baths

The bath house of Valerius

Some wealthier Pompeian houses had their own private baths. One such bathing establishment is to be found in the south–east corner of *insula* 6.

In the first century BC the whole eastern half of the *insula* was one house belonging probably to the family of Valerius Rufus. The property consisted of a large double house with two entrances (2 and 4), two *atria* and a large garden. The house was built on a slope. (There is a drop of nearly four metres between the north and south sides of the *insula*.) About 50 BC the garden was dug away levelling it with the street on the south side. A portico was built surrounding the garden with the bath house attached to its eastern corridor. The surplus earth was then used to raise the level of the garden. This left the floor of the portico three metres below the surface of the garden. Above the north corridor a summer *triclinium* was constructed overlooking the garden (see p. 38).

The bathrooms

At the left side of the illustration is a large vaulted hall. Next to the hall is the first room of the bath house – the changing room (*apodyterium*). This led to the cold bathroom (*frigidarium*). Beyond this was the warm room (*tepidarium*). At the end was the hot room (*caldarium*) with the boiler room (*praefurnium*) next to it. Both the hot and warm rooms were heated by hot air circulated under the floor. The bathing routine and heating methods are discussed on pages 62 to 67.

A change of owner

In the first century AD there was an economic crisis. When the earthquake struck in 62 the whole area was badly damaged and the bath house ruined. The Valerius family were unable to afford the repairs so they sold the eastern half of their house with the portico and baths.

The new owner was probably called Marcus Lucretius. He put in a stairway joining the portico to his side of the house (it can be seen on the right). We do not know whether he intended to restore the bath house. Most of the town was in ruins. Living accommodation was probably given priority. Most of the public buildings had not been restored. When the eruption came the portico was being used only as a wine cellar.

The day of the eruption

When Vesuvius erupted the members of Lucretius's household took shelter in the portico. As the ashes and pumice began to pile up they realized that they might be trapped there. They managed to get out into the garden but here they were overcome by the poisonous fumes. The excavators found about a dozen bodies in the garden including the couple on the right and a baby in its mother's arms.

Below: The bath house at the back of the house of Valerius Rufus. The bathrooms were built on the east side of the semi-underground portico that surrounded the garden. The rooms from the right are: the boiler room, the hot bathroom, the warm room, the cold bathroom and the changing room. The large room at the end is not part of the bath complex.

Plaster casts of two of the many bodies which were found in the garden. This couple brings home to us the pathetic scene as the dying struggled to breathe in the poisonous atmosphere. This young girl has buried her face in the man's clothing. Could this be Lucretius and his daughter Lucretia?

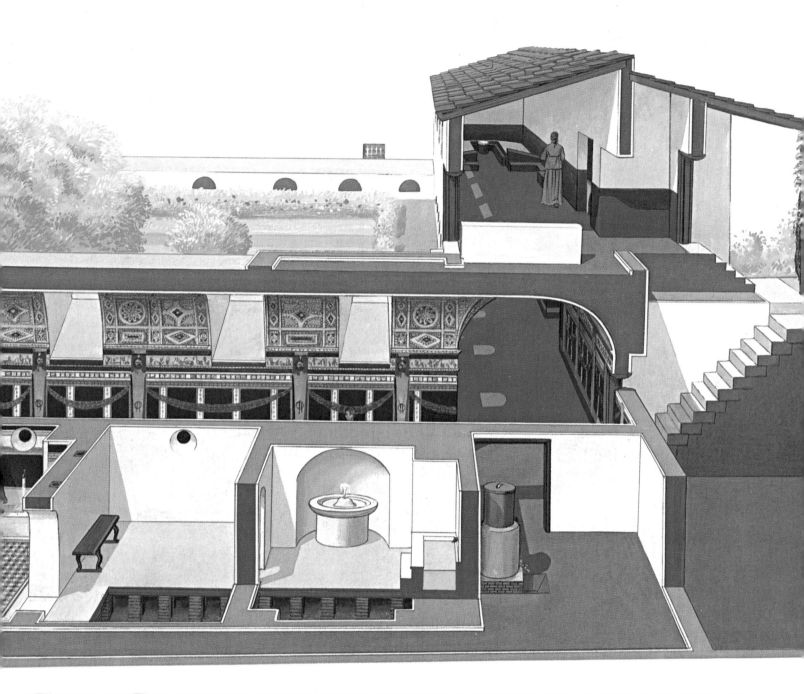

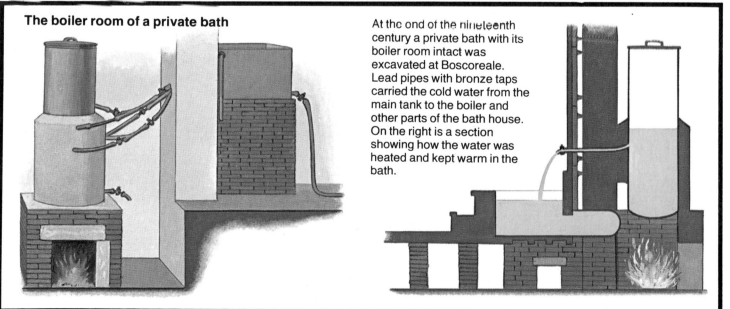

The boiler room of a private bath

At the end of the nineteenth century a private bath with its boiler room intact was excavated at Boscoreale. Lead pipes with bronze taps carried the cold water from the main tank to the boiler and other parts of the bath house. On the right is a section showing how the water was heated and kept warm in the bath.

The street

The via dell'Abbondanza where it passes the north side of region I, *insula* 6.

The second entrance from the right is the ironmongers.

The third and fourth are the tavern and bar and the fifth is the laundry and cloth-finishing shop.

The commercial life of Pompeii

The traders

It is hard for us to imagine when we look at the deserted streets of Pompeii that this was once a harbour town bustling with sailors and foreign merchants. Pompeii was the import and export centre of southern Campania for six hundred years. The people from towns further inland brought their produce here, the touts and confidence tricksters would have come looking for a quick profit. This influx of outsiders is reflected in the almost unbelievable number of taverns, bars and shops that lined Pompeii's streets. There are far more than could be needed by the mere eight to ten thousand inhabitants of the town. There are bars (*thermopolia*) in practically every *insula*. In *insula* 6 and the streets that surround it there are five bars and two taverns.

Life along the high street

To get an idea of street life let us examine one short stretch of road. The picture on the right shows the main east–west street of Pompeii (via dell' Abbondanza) where it runs along the north side of *insula* 6. Along the south side of this street (see p. 24) were a bronzesmith, a laundry and cloth-finishing factory (fullers), a tavern with bar attached, an ironmonger's and three other shops of uncertain use. This picture shows the other side of the street. The area has not yet been excavated. Only the facade has been uncovered.

In the foreground is an inn with a *thermopolium* on the ground floor and rooms above. All the pieces shown in the picture were actually found on the counter. The inn was owned by a woman called Asellina. The names of three chambermaids, Aegle, Maria and Zmyrina, who sold their favours, are painted on the wall outside.

A little further down the street is a wayside shrine with paintings of the gods to whom it was dedicated. Sacrifices would have been offered daily on the small altar. These wayside shrines are found all over Pompeii. In front of the shrine is a public fountain.

Across the side street is the entrance of a workshop where felt was made. Over the door are portraits of four gods. On the left side is a painting of Venus, the patroness of Pompeii. Practically all the commercial premises along the front of this *insula* were involved in cloth manufacture such as dyeing and linen weaving. The laundry and fullers in *insula* 6 (no. 7) which is directly opposite must have been part of this group. All these shops and workshops would have been operated by slaves and managed by freedmen.

The north side of the via dell' Abbondanza opposite region I, *insula* 6.

The shops

The main shopping centre

The main commercial area of Pompeii was the forum. This was the centre of government, business and law. In a town like Pompeii where commerce was its life, the three were sometimes indistinguishable. On the west side of the forum was the basilica. This was a sort of combination of the stock exchange and law courts. Outside, under the colonnade, many small traders set up their stalls. At the north-east corner there was an enclosed area with a fish market in the centre and other stalls around the outside. This was the main shopping centre of the town.

Street-side shops

Shops were not restricted to the forum. There is hardly a street without its share of shops. Wherever the public congregated daily, as at the baths, the whole outer facade of the building was turned over to shops.

Food shops had masonry counters with large earthenware pots *(dolia)* set into them (see overleaf). Grain, dried fruit and liquids were kept in these pots. Meat and poultry were suspended from a bar hung in the entrance. Other shops probably had a table or wooden counter in the entrance.

Many bronze scales have been found. They are identical to those used in Naples today. They consist of a pan and hook for holding the purchase, a crossbar from which the pan and hook are suspended, and a weight which is moved along the bar until it balances. The weights are marked off along the bar.

Shuttered, barred and locked

The entrances to shops were about two to three metres wide. On one side they had a door. The rest of the area was closed by interlocking planks of wood which were slid along a groove in the stone threshold (see right). There must have been a similar groove in the lintel. When all the planks had been put in, the door was closed locking them in position. A plaster cast of such a shutter can be seen in the via dell' Abbondanza immediately opposite *insula* 6.

The shutters could be locked by two bars which were passed through rings riveted to the planks and embedded in the door jambs. These were then locked together so that they could not be pulled out.

The shop of Verus the bronzesmith

On the right is a reconstruction of the shop of the bronzesmith Verus. Like many others, it had living quarters above. These were reached by wooden stairs which ascended from a masonry foundation, which normally formed the first two or three steps. Many bronze lamps and vases were found in the shop. There was also a *groma*, the Roman surveying instrument, which had been brought in for repair.

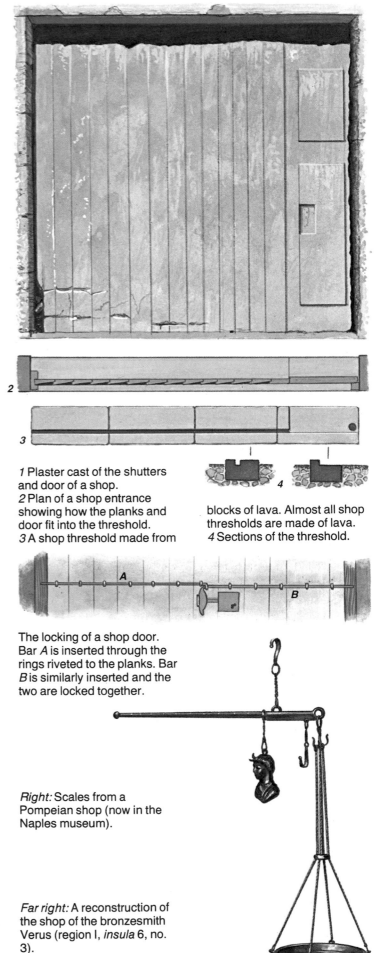

1 Plaster cast of the shutters and door of a shop.
2 Plan of a shop entrance showing how the planks and door fit into the threshold.
3 A shop threshold made from blocks of lava. Almost all shop thresholds are made of lava.
4 Sections of the threshold.

The locking of a shop door. Bar *A* is inserted through the rings riveted to the planks. Bar *B* is similarly inserted and the two are locked together.

Right: Scales from a Pompeian shop (now in the Naples museum).

Far right: A reconstruction of the shop of the bronzesmith Verus (region I, *insula* 6, no. 3).

Bars and taverns

The bars

Bars *(thermopolia)* which sold hot drinks were often no more than tiny rooms opening on to the street. Inside was a masonry counter and an oven. Large earthenware jars *(dolia)* were embedded in the counter. These contained food. A few stone covers for the counter jars have been found. No doubt there were many more made of wood. The counter was sometimes painted but more often it was decorated with irregularly shaped fragments of coloured marble.

The *thermopolium* of Asellina (see far right and page 53) is the most complete example of a bar to be discovered at Pompeii. Many jugs and dishes were found on the counter. These include two terracotta flasks in the form of a cock and a fox. The small dishes, including the one on the tripod, imply that hot snacks were served. At the back is a kettle embedded in the counter. This was hermetically sealed when the ashes came down. When it was uncovered 1,832 years later, the water that was being heated before being mixed with the wine, was still inside. Like so many other bars and taverns, this had guest rooms above.

The love of a slave girl

No bar provided seating. As the customers sipped their drinks they often scribbled on the walls. Opposite the south-east corner of *insula* 6 is another inn with a *thermopolium* attached. Here a weaver called Successus vied with his rival Severus for the heart of a beautiful slave girl named Iris. Their bitter duel is fought out in words scratched on the door posts of the *thermopolium:*

'The weaver Successus loves Iris, the slave of the innkeeper's wife. She doesn't think much of him but he tries to make her feel sorry for him,' wrote Severus. The angry Successus is moved to reply:

'Envious — outbursts of rage! Don't you try to take over from someone who is better looking than you, who knows how to do it and is better endowed.' But Severus gets the final word:

'I have spoken and written — you love Iris but she doesn't care for you — Severus to Successus.'

The taverns

Taverns were usually small. The one attached to the house of Julia Felix (region II, *insula* 4, no 7) has only three tables, and could seat a maximum of twenty-one people. The picture at the centre bottom shows the inside of a tiny tavern at Herculaneum. Here, although the counter has collapsed, the trellis screen behind which the diners sat has survived. Above the diners is a mezzanine floor where *amphorae* were stored. The dining area is only 1.7 by 2.7 metres and could hardly have held more than one table.

Above: A bar showing the counter decorated with fragments of coloured marble.
Right: A section of the counter to show the large earthenware jar *(dolium)* set into it.

Left: A stone cover for the counter jar.

Below: A bar in the via dell' Abbondanza. On the rear wall is a shrine to the household gods *(lararium)* (region I, insula 8, no. 8).

1 A mortar used for grinding down or pulping food.
2 Part of a bronze tray.
3 Top half of a quern used for grinding corn into flour.

4, 5, 6 Bronze cooking vessels, all found on the counter of a bar in Herculaneum.

Above: The inn of Asellina. The ground floor was a *thermoplium* where snacks and hot drinks were served. The stairs lead to the upper floor where there were guest rooms.

Left: A very small tavern in Herculaneum. It is remarkable for the wonderful state of preservation of the woodwork.

Below: The tavern and bar attached to the house of Julia Felix (region II, *insula* 4, no. 7). The roof has been removed to show the inside. The tables and benches are made of masonry. This tavern offered its customers the choice of reclining or sitting upright to eat.

The fullers and launderers

Left: A wall painting showing a fuller's press. The remains of a double press like this were found in the entrance to the *fullonica* of Stephanus.

The laundry of Stephanus

This laundry (no.7 in *insula* 6) was in fact a *fullonica*. There is no direct English translation for this word. Although it was a laundry its prime job was fulling — the finishing of manufactured cloth.

The *fullonica* of Stephanus (shown reconstructed on the right) was a converted house. The various bedrooms, the *atrium* and the *tablinum* can easily be identified. So also can the area at the back which was once a peristyle garden. This *atrium* is the only one yet discovered with a flat roof. The *impluvium* has been converted into a large vat. The wall between the entrance and one front bedroom has been demolished to make way for a shop-type entrance.

When the building was excavated in 1911 the entrance was still shuttered and locked. Only the side door was open. Behind the shutters a body was found still clutching a bag of money. It contained $1089\frac{1}{2}$ sesterces. Was this the last takings of the *fullonica* or had a passing stranger, carrying his savings, taken refuge behind the door and died there?

The fulling process

The fulling process was very complicated and is best explained using the reconstruction drawing. It is not known for certain where each process took place. Some of the rooms have been allocated at random.

First the cloth was examined for faults which were mended and any bits of fluff were removed. It was then soaked in urine to stiffen it. Urine was collected outside the door in a pot which passers-by were asked to use. Similar pots were placed at street corners. The Emperor Vespasian (AD 69-79) put a tax on this with the result that public urinals got the nickname of Vespasiani. The stiffened cloth was washed with fuller's earth or other cleansing agents to remove grease. The process can be seen on a Pompeian painting (see top right) where the cloth is being trodden in basins. These treading bowls can be seen beyond the large vats (*A,B,C*) at the rear of the *fullonica*.

The fabric was now taken to a room behind the old *tablinum* (*3*). Here it was stretched and beaten to make the surface even before being rewashed in the large vats at the back. The water entered vat *A*. From here it overflowed into vats *B* and *C*. Vat *A* would therefore have the cleanest water. The cloth must have been washed in vats *B* and *C* and rinsed in vat *A*.

Once dry the cloth was taken to room *4* where it was combed to bring up the nap. Next it was moved to room *5*. Here it was brushed and clipped to trim the surface. White woollens were taken up to the roof where they were laid over wooden cages. Sulphur and brimstone were burned underneath them to bleach the cloth. Finally the cloth was taken down to the front room (*1*) where it was flattened in a large press.

Below: A reconstruction of the *fullonica* of Stephanus. Where the numbers are not found on the illustration they can be found on the plan in the corner.
1 Entrance and pressing room
2 Laundry room
3 Beating and stretching room
4 Combing room
5 Brushing and clipping room
6 Toilet
7 Kitchen
A,B,C Washing vats. The treading bowls are on either side of *B*.

Above: A wall painting showing cloth being trampled in vats. This painting gives evidence child labour was used for unpleasant jobs.

Left: The remains of a single press from Herculaneum.

Above: A wall painting showing a girl combing cloth with a carding tool to raise the nap and a man carrying a bleaching frame. In his left hand he is carrying a bucket with sulphur and brimstone used in the bleaching process.

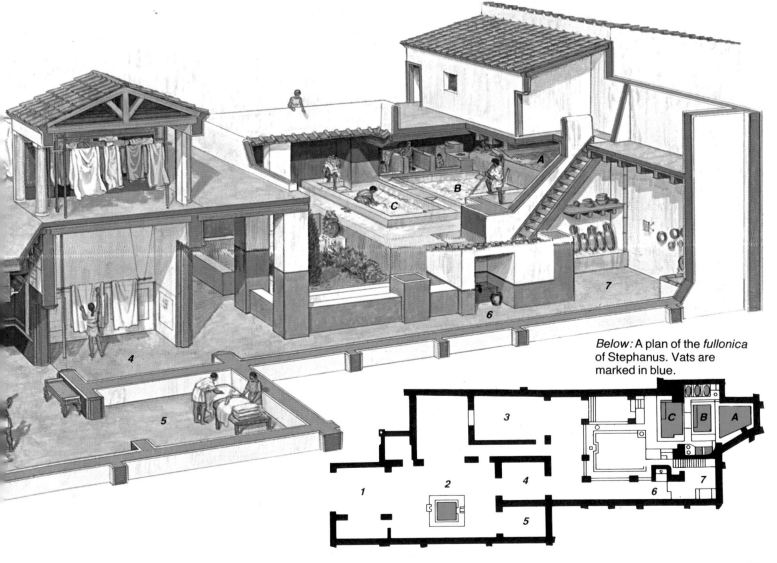

Below: A plan of the *fullonica* of Stephanus. Vats are marked in blue.

The public baths 1

The Stabian baths

There are three large public baths at Pompeii: the Forum baths, the Stabian baths and the central baths, which were still being built at the time of the eruption. The Stabian baths, at the junction of Pompeii's two main streets, the via dell'Abbondanza and the via Stabiana, was the largest. They were badly damaged in the earthquake of AD 62. Only the women's quarters were in use at the time of the eruption.

Exercise and swimming

The Stabian baths were only two blocks away from *insula* 6. Most of its inhabitants would have taken their daily bath there. On the right is a reconstruction of the baths. The men went in by the main entrance (*1*). This was on the south side under the gabled roof on the left of the illustration. There was a second entrance for men on the west side (*2*). These led to an open exercise area (*palaestra*). To the left of the entrance at the far end of the colonnade was a changing room (*3*).

After undressing the men could either exercise or take a swim. They took this exercise in the *palaestra*. Several games were played here. The most popular was a form of bowling which was played along the paved 'alley' (*4*). At the far end was a room where the games were kept. Next to this was the office of the baths' manager (*5*). On the right side of the illustration is the north block. The public toilets were here (*7*). Above these was a huge water tank (*8*). In earlier days it was filled by a treadmill operating two pot-garland water wheels which drew water from a well. Later it was supplied by the aqueduct.

When they had worked up a good sweat from their exercise the men returned to the changing room where they were scraped down with strigils and massaged. If they then wished to take a swim they walked through a shallow bath (*9*) to clean their feet before plunging into the swimming pool (*10*). After this they might visit the heated baths (*11-15*).

The Stabian baths seen from the east. Part of the roof has been cut away to show the inside.

1 Main entrance	*13* Cold bathroom
2 West entrance	*14* Warm room
3 Changing room	*15* Hot room
4 Bowling alley	*16* Boiler room
5 Manager's office	*17* Hot tank
6 Entrance to north block	*18* Warm tank
7 Public toilets	*19* Cold tank
8 Water tank and treadmill	*20* Main furnace
9 Shallow bath	*21* Draught fire
10 Swimming bath	*22* Servants' waiting room
11-15 The men's baths	*23-28 The women's baths*
11 Entrance hall	*23* West entrance
12 Changing room	*24* East entrance
	25 Changing room
	26 Cold bath
	27 Warm room
	28 Hot room

The public baths 2

The heated bathrooms

The heated bathrooms were in the east wing. The men's baths were at the south end of the wing and the women's at the north end.

Both the men's and the women's quarters had three rooms. A hot room (*caldarium*) next to the boiler room. A warm room (*tepidarium*) and a changing room (*apodyterium*). The men's quarters also included a small circular room with a cold plunge bath (*frigidarium*). The women's quarters had no *frigidarium* but there was a cold bath in the changing room.

After removing their clothes in the changing room the bathers could either have a quick cold dip or go straight into the warm room. This room was heated to a constant temperature. It served as an acclimatizing room allowing the body to get used to the change of temperature between the changing room and the hot bathroom. This was particularly important when leaving the hot room in the winter.

The heating system (hypocaust)

In the boiler room (*16*) were three large tanks for cold, warm and hot water. There was a furnace beneath the hot tank which also heated the warm tank next to it. The cold tank was on a solid masonry base. The hot air from the furnace passed through holes at the bottom of the walls into the two hot bathrooms. Here it circulated under the floor which was raised up on small rectangular pillars. It also flowed up inside the walls and across the ceiling. After circulating round the hot rooms it passed through holes at the bottom of the walls to heat the warm rooms in the same way. It then passed out through small holes in the end walls of the warm rooms: there are two of these exhaust holes in the west wall of the women's *tepidarium* and four in the east wall of the men's. Behind the bath in the men's *tepidarium* is a small fireplace. This was a draught fire which was used to draw through the hot air.

Plan of the Stabian baths
30 Palaestra
31 Well
S Shops
T Bar

Above: the north-east corner of the *palaestra* of the Stabian baths showing the colonnade and the entrance to the north block.

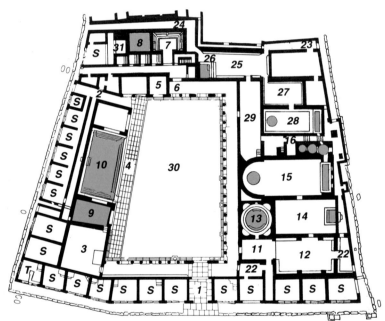

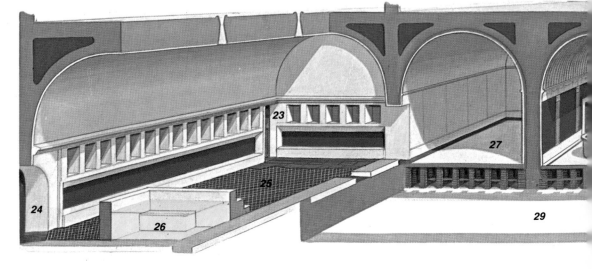

Right: A cut-away section of the bath-block of the Stabian baths.
11-15 The men's baths
11 Entrance hall
12 Changing room
13 Cold bathroom
14 Warm room
15 Hot room
16 Boiler room
17 Hot tank
25-29 The women's baths
25 Changing room
26 Cold bath
27 Warm room
28 Hot room
29 Possible exercise area

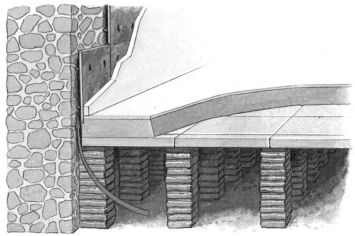

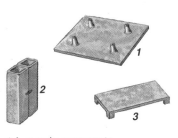

1 A *tegula mammata* showing the four nipples.
2 Box tiles *(tubuli).*
3 A tile with corner supports. *2* and *3* can be used instead of *tegulae mammatae.*

Above: The hypocaust system. The floor, made of square paving stones, is supported on small brick columns. It is covered by a layer of mortar and then surfaced with a mosaic paving. Nipple tiles *(tegulae mammatae)* are nailed to the wall. The nipples hold the tiles away from the wall leaving a space behind them. The surface is then plastered over. The hot air flows between the brick columns and up the space between the tiles and the wall.

Above: A reconstruction of the men's changing room. The rectangular niches in the wall are for the bathers' clothing.

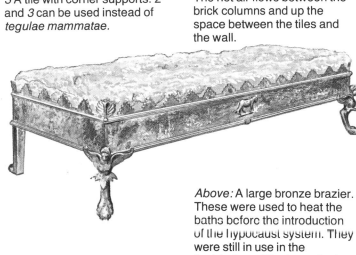

Above: A large bronze brazier. These were used to heat the baths before the introduction of the hypocaust system. They were still in use in the *tepidarium* of the forum baths in AD 79.

The public baths 3

The women's bathrooms

The women's quarters were reached by two corridors, one from the west and one from the east side (see p.63, *23* and *24*). Women coming from *insula* 6 would have entered by the east entrance in the via Stabiana. These two corridors led only to the changing room. It was impossible to get from these corridors to any other part of the building.

Originally the women's quarters were entirely isolated from the rest of the complex. Later a doorway was put in giving access to the *palaestra* from the long hall (*29*). This hall may have been the women's exercise area. The door to the *palaestra* was probably put in only after the earthquake when the men's baths were out of action. Alternatively it might have been a service entrance which was kept locked during working hours.

In contrast to the ruined state of the men's baths the women's baths are in excellent condition. The changing room still had its roof intact when it was excavated. Although the roof of the hot room had collapsed most of the room is in a good state. The nipple tiles are still on the walls and most of the decoration, including part of the ceiling, has survived.

The hot bath

At the east end of the women's hot room is a bath (*alveus*) made of masonry faced with marble. Not only is the bath itself intact but so is the system for keeping the water hot. At the right end of the bath (see right *1–3*) there is a semi-circular opening. Inside this is a half cylinder made of bronze. This container sits immediately above the hypocaust channel leading from the furnace (see right *3*). It is set slightly lower than the bath. As the water in the bath cools it sinks and so ends up in the half cylinder where it reheats and rises thus keeping a permanent circulation of hot water in the bath. A similar system operated in the men's hot room but today it is completely in ruins.

The bath held about eight people. Those who wished to bathe on their own could use individual bronze tubs. The remains of one of these was found in this room. At the other end of the room was the *labrum*, a shallow wash basin made of white marble.

Taking a bath

Normally bathers would be rubbed with ointments in the warm room before entering the hot room. Here they would sweat in the intense heat. The room was so hot that they had to wear special clogs to protect the feet from the hot floor. After sweating they would take a hot bath followed by a cold plunge and then return to the hot room for a second sweat. Before leaving the heated rooms they would be rubbed down again with ointments as a protection against the cold.

1 The women's hot bath. The water heater is at the far end.

2 A section of the hot bath.

3 A section of the water heater. The blue arrow shows the flow of the colder water from the bath (A) down into the half cylinder (B). The red arrow shows the flow of the reheated water back into the bath.

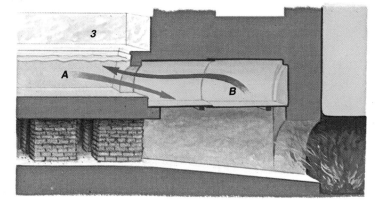

The public toilet in the Stabian baths

Public toilets are found wherever people gathered, such as the Forum, the theatre and the baths. The example in the Stabian baths is a typical Roman latrine. Along three sides of the room is a deep trough (see the reconstruction below). This sloped downwards so that the water entering at the higher end flowed out at the lower. Above this were seats supported by blocks of stone set into the wall. No remains of the wooden seats were found. However stone seats have been found at several sites. These have small holes in the top which are extended to form U-shaped holes along the front. About 30cm in front of the seats is a shallow channel, also with flowing water. The people cleansed themselves with a sponge on the end of a stick which they used through the U-shaped hole and then rinsed it in the shallow channel.

Public toilets

1 Section of the stone toilet seats from Lepcis Magna in North Africa.
2 Detail of a stone seat.

Below: a reconstruction of the public toilet in the Stabian baths. No trace of the wooden seats remains.

3 A sponge stick.

Above: A reconstruction of the women's hot room in the Stabian baths. In the foreground is the wash basin *(labrum)* and in the background the bath *(alveus)*.

Left: Two bathroom shoes with thick wooden soles to protect the feet from the heated floor. These were found at Vindolanda on Hadrian's Wall in England.

1 A ring with three strigils, a dish and an ointment jar.
2 An ointment jar
3 A strigil
These were all found at Pompeii. Strigils were used to scrape off sweat and grime.

The theatre

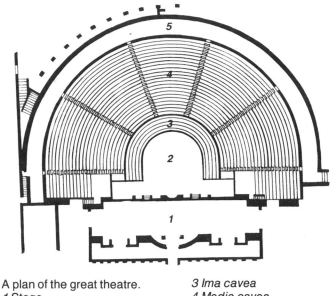

A plan of the great theatre.
1 Stage
2 Orchestra
3 Ima cavea
4 Media cavea
5 Summa cavea

The places of entertainment

There were two main centres of entertainment at Pompeii: the theatres near the Stabian Gate and the amphitheatre at the east end of the town. The theatre was never as popular as the amphitheatre whose bloody shows appealed to people's most primitive emotions. Even so, the many graffiti commenting on the theatre and the large number of theatrical paintings found in houses show that it had a great following.

There were two theatres: a large open building holding about 5,000 people and a smaller one built next to it. The small theatre, which was roofed over, held only about 1,200 people. It was used for concerts and recitals.

The large theatre

The large theatre was built into a natural hollow in the hillside. The seating area (*cavea*) was in the shape of a broad horseshoe with the stage built across its open end. The space enclosed between the seats and the stage was called the orchestra. The seating was divided into three sections. Nearest the orchestra were four wide ledges (*ima cavea*). The musicians and the town council put their seats here. Behind this were twenty rows of stone seats (*media cavea*). The seats were like large steps about 40cm high and 65 to 70cm wide, unfortunately only a few fragments of these seats remain. One has numbered places marked on it. These allow only 40cm per person. The *media cavea* was divided into seven sections. Its area was enclosed by a corridor which gave access to the seven sections. Four more rows of seats (*summa cavea*) were perched above the corridor. The whole seating area was surrounded by a wall, near the top of which were sockets which held wooden posts. These supported a huge canvas awning which was stretched over the audience and attached to the roof of the stage. This awning protected the audience from the sun. During intervals in the performance, scented water was sometimes sprinkled on the audience. It was announced on posters when this was to happen.

The actors

Actors in ancient times caused the same hysteria and hero worship as they do today. Their praises are scribbled on walls: 'Actius, darling of the people, come back quickly.' One actor, Paris, is the subject of many graffiti: 'Paris, pearl of the stage', 'Paris sweet darling'. He even had a fan club — 'The comrades of Paris'.

On the stage actors wore masks. These were caricatures of the characters being portrayed. There were comic masks with great grinning mouths and tragic masks with gaping mouths. The repertoire of these actors included tragedies, mimes, comedies and farces. These farces, called *atellanae,* were enormously popular.

Above: A mosaic showing actors preparing to go on stage.

Below: A mosaic showing a tragic mask.

68

Above: A section through the middle of the great theatre showing the western half. The *summa cavea (5)* collapsed during the earthquake and had not been rebuilt at the time of the eruption. There is room for only four rows of seats. Today there is no trace of the top three rows of the *media cavea* but these are clearly visible on nineteenth-century prints.

1 Stage
2 Orchestra
3 *Ima cavea*
4 *Media cavea*
5 *Summa cavea*
6 Corridor
7 West entrance to orchestra

Above: A mosaic showing street musicians.

Below: The small theatre. This intimate theatre was only used for concerts and recitals.

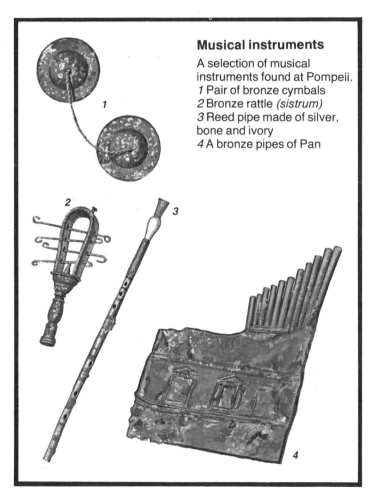

Musical instruments

A selection of musical instruments found at Pompeii.
1 Pair of bronze cymbals
2 Bronze rattle *(sistrum)*
3 Reed pipe made of silver, bone and ivory
4 A bronze pipes of Pan

The amphitheatre

A place to die

Amphitheatres (literally double theatres) were designed specifically to stage exhibition killings. Such 'games' had been popular in southern Italy long before they became so in Rome. The main training schools were at Capua, forty kilometres north of Pompeii. Many gladiatorial traditions probably originated in the highlands of southern Italy. One type of gladiator was called Samnite after these hill people. The design of much of the armour discovered at Pompeii can be clearly traced back to its Samnite origin.

The amphitheatre was oval. It was divided into three parts like the theatre. The *ima cavea* (five rows of seats) was nearest the arena, the *media cavea* (twelve rows) was in the middle and the *summa cavea* (eighteen rows) was at the top. It could seat about 20,000 people. There were two main entrances to the arena, one at the north and one at the south end. There was also a narrow passage on the west side, the death gate, where the dead were dragged out.

A riot in the arena

During the games the spectators sometimes became very violent. The painting on the right recalls a scene that took place in AD 59. The amphitheatre was filled with people from Pompeii and many of its neighbouring towns. (This must have been normal as the amphitheatre can seat twice the total population of Pompeii.) In the crowd was a group from the town of Nuceria. During the games fighting started between the Pompeians and Nucerians. Many of the Nucerians were killed or wounded. They appealed to Rome and the Emperor closed down the arena for ten years.

The gladiators

Gladiators were mainly slaves or criminals. The life expectancy of a gladiator could be reckoned in weeks rather than years. Most of the poor wretches acquired by the training schools were simply used for exhibition killings by veterans. However ghastly the prospects of a man sent to the arena might seem, if he could survive long enough to get the necessary experience, a very different future was open to him. If actors were loved then gladiators were worshipped. A popular gladiator could become wealthy. The crowd would not allow him to be killed. In the end he would gain his discharge from the arena and his freedom.

The gladiators' barracks were in the *palaestra* behind the great theatre. Many pieces of armour were found here. When the detention room was excavated the bodies of four gladiators were found. They had not been released when their trainers fled. A further eighteen skeletons were found in the barracks, including a woman wearing a wealth of jewellery. Perhaps some patrician lady came here in search of her lover.

Above: A painting found in a house near the theatre (now in the Naples museum). It shows the riot in the amphitheatre in AD 59 when several people were killed.

Above: The outside of the amphitheatre seen from the west. In the centre are steps going up to the *summa cavea.*

Below: The inside of the amphitheatre seen from the north-west.

Above: A painting showing Samnite gladiators found in a tomb outside the Vesuvius Gate.

Above: The gladiators' barracks and exercise area *(palaestra)* seen from the large theatre.

Below: The remains of iron stocks found in the detention room of the gladiators' barracks.

Gladiatorial equipment

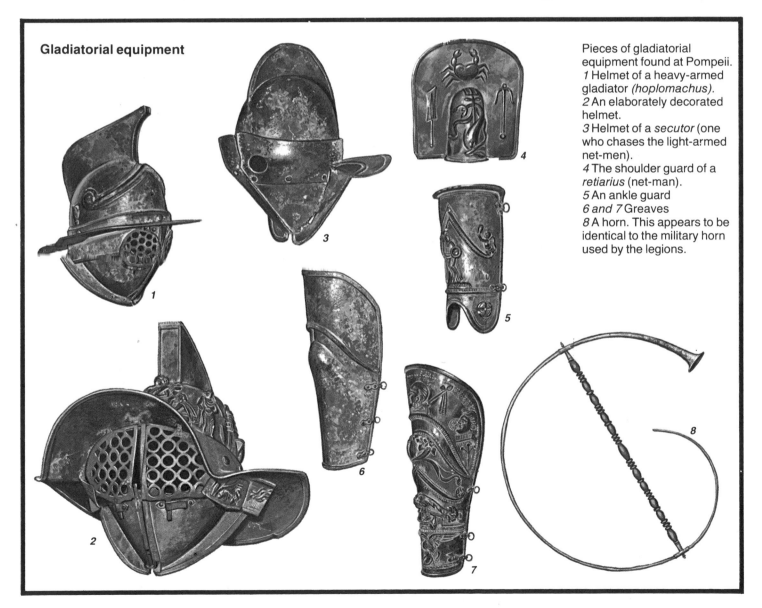

Pieces of gladiatorial equipment found at Pompeii.
1 Helmet of a heavy-armed gladiator *(hoplomachus)*.
2 An elaborately decorated helmet.
3 Helmet of a *secutor* (one who chases the light-armed net-men).
4 The shoulder guard of a *retiarius* (net-man).
5 An ankle guard
6 and 7 Greaves
8 A horn. This appears to be identical to the military horn used by the legions.

In the arena

The admirers of the gladiators

Many of Pompeii's graffiti were scribbled by the gladiators' admirers. One reads: 'Twenty pairs of gladiators provided by Decimus Lucretius Satrius Valens, permanent priest of Nero, son of the Emperor, and ten pairs provided by Decimus Lucretius Valens, his son, will fight at Pompeii 8-12 April. There will be a really big hunt and the awnings will be up.' On one side is written: 'Aemilius Celer wrote this all alone by the light of the moon.' Aemilius Celer the phantom scribber, was responsible for many of Pompeii's graffiti. Another speaks of a teenage idol: 'Celadus, glory of the girls, heart-throb of the girls.' Others tell of the careers of gladiators: 'Auctus of the Julian school has won fifty times.' 'Quintus Petronius Octavius has gained his discharge after thirty-three fights.'

Types of gladiator

There were many types of gladiator. Samnites have already been mentioned. Thracians, too, were named after their place of origin. Some were named after their armour, such as the *hoplomachus* (heavy-armed) and the *myrmillo,* from the symbol of a fish (*mormyrus*) on his helmet. Others got their names from the way they fought. The *retiarius* fought with a trident and net (*rete*) The *secutor* (follower) chased the net-man. There were chariot fighters dressed as ancient Britons and various types who fought animals (*bestiarii*).

The bloody games

The games opened with a parade of the gladiators. They entered the arena by the north gate and left by the south. The show started with mock fights to warm up the spectators. The gladiators then entered the arena two at a time. During the fights an orchestra played and the crowd screamed their encouragement to the contestants. The fight went on until one of the gladiators was severely wounded. Then trumpets sounded and the referee restrained the victor. The wounded man held up a finger of his left hand as a plea for mercy. In theory it was up to the organizer of the games to decide his fate but in reality the crowd decided. If he had fought well they would reprieve him, if not, the victor would be given the order to finish the job.

After the kill an official dressed as Charun the Etruscan demon of the underworld, clubbed the vanquished gladiator to make sure he was dead. He was then dragged through the death gate with hooks.

After the contests the results were posted. 'Pugnax, a Thracian of the Neronian school with three fights to his credit, won. Murranus, a *myrmillo* of the Neronian school with three fights, was killed. Cycnus, a *hoplomachus* of the Julian school with eight fights, won. Atticus, a Thracian with fourteen fights, was reprieved.' Atticus had obviously fought well.

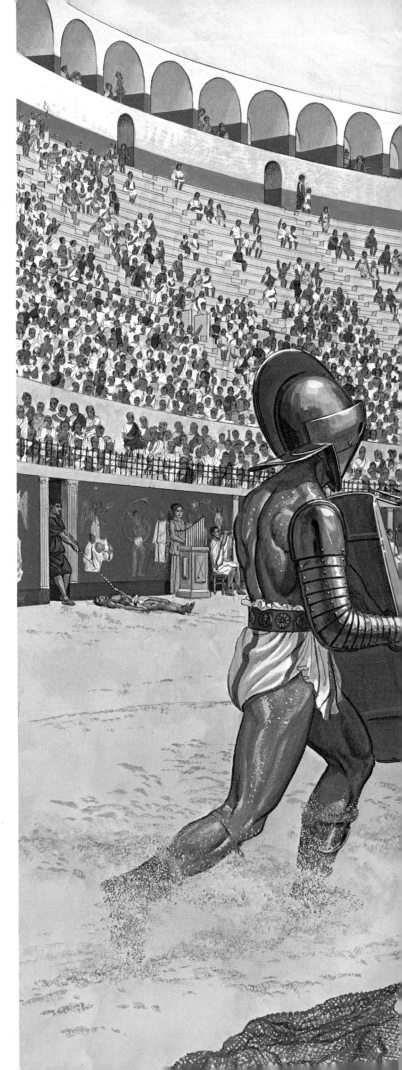

A gladiatorial contest in the amphitheatre at Pompeii. In the foreground is a contest between a *secutor* and a *retiarius*. The *retiarius* is wounded and has lost his net. Now only his speed can save him. An official dressed as Charun, the Etruscan demon of the underworld, waits in the background. He may be called upon to club the vanquished gladiator to death.

Maps

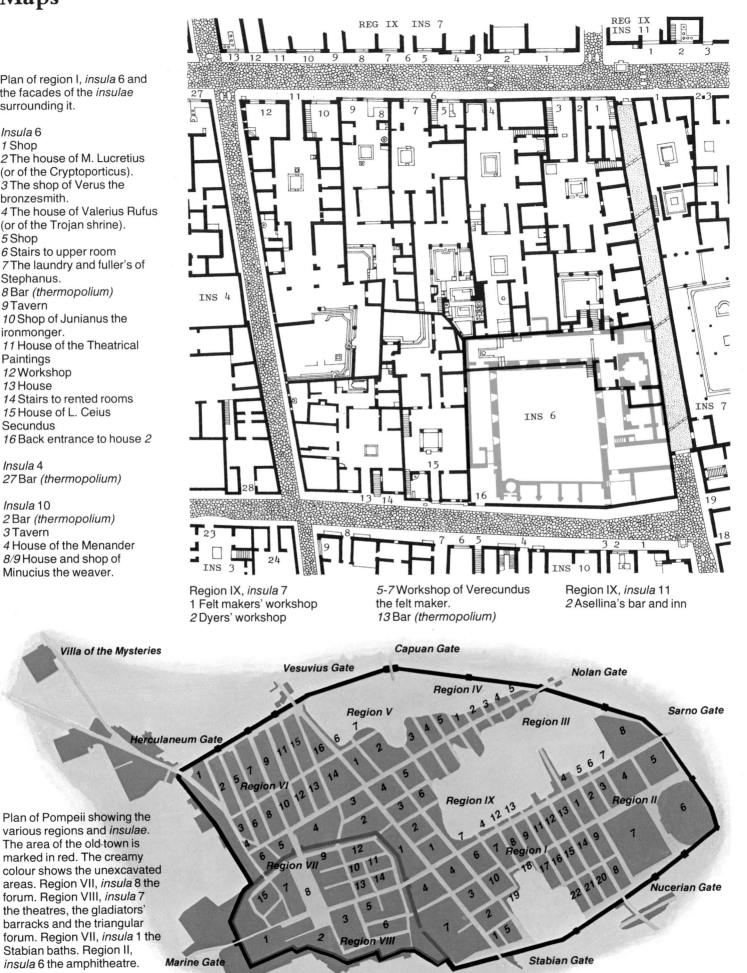

Plan of region I, *insula* 6 and the facades of the *insulae* surrounding it.

Insula 6
1 Shop
2 The house of M. Lucretius (or of the Cryptoporticus).
3 The shop of Verus the bronzesmith.
4 The house of Valerius Rufus (or of the Trojan shrine).
5 Shop
6 Stairs to upper room
7 The laundry and fuller's of Stephanus.
8 Bar *(thermopolium)*
9 Tavern
10 Shop of Junianus the ironmonger.
11 House of the Theatrical Paintings
12 Workshop
13 House
14 Stairs to rented rooms
15 House of L. Ceius Secundus
16 Back entrance to house *2*

Insula 4
27 Bar *(thermopolium)*

Insula 10
2 Bar *(thermopolium)*
3 Tavern
4 House of the Menander
8/9 House and shop of Minucius the weaver.

REG IX INS 7

REG IX INS 11

INS 4

INS 6

INS 7

INS 3

INS 10

Region IX, *insula* 7
1 Felt makers' workshop
2 Dyers' workshop

5-7 Workshop of Verecundus the felt maker.
13 Bar *(thermopolium)*

Region IX, *insula* 11
2 Asellina's bar and inn

Villa of the Mysteries

Capuan Gate

Vesuvius Gate

Nolan Gate

Region IV

Region V

Sarno Gate

Region III

Herculaneum Gate

Region VI

Region IX

Region I

Region II

Region VII

Region VIII

Marine Gate

Stabian Gate

Nucerian Gate

Plan of Pompeii showing the various regions and *insulae*. The area of the old town is marked in red. The creamy colour shows the unexcavated areas. Region VII, *insula* 8 the forum. Region VIII, *insula* 7 the theatres, the gladiators' barracks and the triangular forum. Region VII, *insula* 1 the Stabian baths. Region II, *insula* 6 the amphitheatre.

Glossary

Aedileship There were two aediles who were elected annually. They were junior magistrates whose main responsibility was the upkeep of public buildings.

Amphorae Large earthenware jars used mainly for storing liquids such as wine.

Architrave The horizontal slab of stone or timber laid across the top of two columns.

Atrium The main reception court of an Italic house.

Cicero Marcus Tullius, 106-43 BC. Famous Roman orator and statesman.

Coffered Decorated with sunken panels. A coffered ceiling, for example, is made up of a grid of sunken panels.

Decurions A non-elected body of town councillors.

Duumvir One of two senior elected magistrates.

Fiorelli Guiseppe, 1807-1882, guerrilla leader who took part in the unification of Italy which was achieved in 1860. As Professor of Archaeology at Naples he was responsible for the main excavations at Pompeii.

Forum The market place and centre of government, law and business in a Roman town.

Fuller One who 'finishes' newly woven cloth.

Fuller's earth A type of clay used to remove grease from newly woven cloth.

Insula An area at Pompeii surrounded by streets, equivalent to a 'block' in a present-day town.

Italic Native to Italy.

Lava The molten rock that erupts from a volcano.

Lintel A horizontal beam or stone used to support the wall above a doorway.

Patrician Aristocrat.

Petronius A senior magistrate under the Emperor Nero (AD 54-68). He wrote a satirical novel called *The Satyricon*.

Plan view Seen from above.

Pliny the Elder (Gaius Plinius Secundus) AD 23-79. A senior Roman magistrate. He wrote a large volume on natural history. He was appointed admiral of the Roman fleet at Misenum by the Emperor Vespasian. He was killed during the eruption of Vesuvius in AD 79.

Pliny the Younger (Gaius Plinius Caecilius Secundus) AD c.62-c.114, nephew of Pliny the Elder. He wrote two letters to the historian Tacitus giving an account of the eruption of Vesuvius.

Pompey the Great (Gnaeus Pompeius Magnus) 106-48 BC. Roman general and politician. He led the opposition to Julius Caesar. He was defeated at the battle of Pharsalia in 48 BC.

Pot-garland water-wheel A system of drawing up water using a series of pots strung together.

Pumice A light porous volcanic stone.

Region One of the nine areas into which Pompeii was divided.

Section (view) A view of a building obtained by cutting the building in half to reveal the inside.

Sesterces Roman bronze coins.

Strabo c.64 BC-AD c.21. Greek historian and geographer. His work is a mine of odd and interesting pieces of information.

Tacitus Cornelius AD c.55-c.120. Roman historian who wrote a history of the early Roman empire.

Vespasian (Titus Flavius Vespasianus) Roman emperor AD 69-79. He died shortly before the eruption of Vesuvius. He was succeeded by his son Titus.

Index